Sedona's RENÉ at Tlaquepaque

Sedona's RENÉ at Tlaquepaque

The Chef's Secret Recipes

Walter Paulson

Sedona's René at Tlaquepaque: The Chef's Secret Recipes

Copyright © 2018 Walter Paulson

All rights reserved. No part of this book maybe reproduced or transmitted in any form by any means, electronic or mechanical, including photocopying, digital scanning and recording, or by any information storage and retrieval system, without permission in writing from the publisher.

For more information:
Sedona Publishing
P.O. Box 2266
Sedona, Arizona 86339

PUBLISHED 2018 by Sedona Publishing
http://renerestaurantsedona.com/
928.282.9225
walterpaulson825@gmail.com

ISBN: 978-0-9998118-0-1

Library of Congress Control Number: 2018903317

Book design by Sarah E. Holroyd (http://sleepingcatbooks.com)
Copy editor K. D. Kragen, KaveDragen Ink LLC, kavedragenink.com
Book Shepherd: Trudy Catterfeld, BookMarketingNext
Front cover photograph by Emmanuelle Geis
Food dishes photographs by Vibhas P.A. Kendzia
Tlaquepaque photographs by Wib Middleton
Walter Paulson portrait drawing on back cover by Libby Caldwell
Oak Creek at Slide Rock painting used by permission of the artist, Alfred Currier
Stock photos licensed by Adobe

Dedication

I would like to dedicate this book to the memory of René Baudat, founder of René at Tlaquepaque. And all the guests of René Restaurant since 1978.

Thank you for your loyalty and support.

Table of Contents

Foreword	xi
Introduction	xiii
Acknowledgements	xv
Sedona, Arizona	xvii
Tlaquepaque	xix
Appetizers	**1**
Ahi Tartar	2
Dungeness Crab Cakes	4
Lobster Martini	5
Mushrooms Neptune	6
Smoked Salmon with Boursin Cheese Sauce on Roesti Potatoes	7
Southwestern Crab Cakes	9
Beef Carpaccio	10
Steak Tartar	11
Gruyère and Parmesan Beignets	12
Cheese Soufflé	13
Domaine Cheese	14
Sautéed Brie with Caramelized Apples	15
English Pea Griddle Cakes	16
Roasted Red Pepper Hummus	18
Soups	**21**
French Onion Soup Gratinee	22
Sweet Corn Soup with Smoked Chili Cream	23
Roasted Butternut Squash Soup with Fig Quenelle	24
Vegetarian Split Pea Soup	25
Lobster Bisque	26
Portobello Bisque	28
Tomato Bisque	29
Sweet Potato Bisque	30
Chilled Vichyssoise	31
Sweet Potato Vichyssoise	32
Chilled Gazpacho	34
Roasted Beet Gazpacho	35
Salads	**37**
Arugula and Roasted Beet Salad	38
Kale and Quinoa Salad	40
Spinach and Tofu Salad	41
Spinach and Wild Mushroom Salad	42
Ahi Salad	43
Salmon Salad	45
Scallop Salad	46
Hearts of Romaine	47
Sautéed Miso Marinated Beef Salad	48

Entrees	**51**
Champagne Veal	52
Fettuccine Bolognese	53
Madame Oak Creek	54
Chicken Crepes	55
Chicken Piccata	57
Southwestern Chicken Cordon Bleu	58
Chicken Marsala	59
Eggs Benedict	60
Eggs Florentine	62
Braised Lamb Shank	64
Roasted Pork Tenderloin with Sun-Dried Cherry Sauce and Creamed Pine Nuts	65
Tenderloin of Beef with Whisky Juniper Berry Sauce	66
Cedar Plank Salmon with Roasted Red Pepper Salsa	67
Rocky Mountain Rainbow Trout Almondine	68
Sautéed Sand Dabs au Meunière	69
Acorn Squash	70
Eggplant Parmesan	71
Wild Mushroom Strudel	73
Portobello Bolognese	74
Seitan Wellington	75
Spaghetti Squash Primavera	78
Tournedos Au Poivre	79
Desserts	**81**
Carrot Cake with Cream Cheese Frosting	82
Flourless Chocolate Torte	83
Goat Cheesecake with Lime Cream and Tropical Fruit Salsa	84
Chocolate Bourbon Pecan Pie	86
Apple Brown Betty	87
Chocolate Mousse	88
Triple Chocolate Mousse Terrine	89
Chocolate Pots de Creme	90
Crème Carmel	91
Vanilla Bean Crème Brûlée	92
Profiteroles	93
Lemon Berry Mille-Feuille	94
Lemon Panna Cotta with Blueberry Sauce	95
Carrot Soufflé with Cream Cheese Sauce	96
Oven Roasted Peaches with Honeyed Ricotta Cheese	98
Banana Soufflé	99
Chocolate Grand Marnier Soufflé	100
Crepes Suzette	101
Bananas Foster	102
Cherries Jubilee	103
Chocolate Cake with Chocolate Mousse Filling and Cream Cheese Frosting	104

Stocks, Sides, Sauces, Dressings   **107**
   Demi-Glace   108
   Chicken Stock   109
   Au Gratin Potatoes   110
   Dauphinoise   111
   Duchess Potatoes   112
   Wild Rice and Mushroom Cakes   113
   Nut Relish   114
   Gluten-Free Flour   115
   Spaghetti Squash   116
   Miso Marinade   117
Seasonal Menu Suggestions   **119**
Index   **120**

Foreword

From his first days in 1993 as the new executive chef René at Tlaquepaque, Walter Paulson proved himself a passionate leader who not only cared about guests' total dining experience but also valued input from his dining room team.

Walter set himself from the start to solve the challenges that arose in the course of guest services. He used his knowledge and experience to make needed changes for sumptuous meals to better serve René's distinguished clientele looking for a tasty repast. His revised menu was a hit, raising the restaurant to a new level of popularity with locals and tourists. With an acute attention to detail, Walter even procured the best coffee available.

René at Tlaquepaque, originally opened by René Baudat in 1978, is a landmark Sedona restaurant nestled within vine covered stucco walls, cobblestone walkways, and magnificent arched entry. Walter came to René from his position as executive chef of L'Auberge de Sedona from 1991-1993. And for the next twenty-five years, Walter has brought to the René team a passion for great food, wine, and service—dressed in an elegant yet relaxed atmosphere.

Taking tried and true recipes guests had come to rely on, Walter breathed new life into them. His love of pure, fresh ingredients, created-from-scratch sauces, and consistency of preparation made his dishes exceptional. His passion for cooking led him on a journey of transforming restaurant trends and lifestyles. He experimented with innovative incorporation of vegetarian, vegan, and gluten free dishes into existing recipes. Known for his creativity and love of research, Walter studied the nuances of various seeds, grains, flours, and vegan arrangements, delighting even the pickiest of eaters.

In Walter's own words, "The dessert is the last taste of a memorable dining experience, and it has to be the best." The rich creamy Chocolate Mousse is a chocolate lover's dream. The decadent Goat-Cheesecake has a subtle balance of sweet and tangy. His profiteroles pâte à choux pastry, filled with a scoop of vanilla or peppermint gelato, is easy to prepare. And don't be intimidated in baking his light and airy Chocolate Grand Marnier Soufflé!

Today, the quality and innovation of recipes added to René's historical European standards are a winning blend! As chef and owner, Walter has established an evolving team of loyal employees that has simply improved the lovely and magical dining experience for their treasured patrons.

Enjoy the adventure of creating warm memories and mouthwatering delicious meals from the recipes of *René at Tlaquepaque*.

Sincerely,
Friends of *René at Tlaquepaque*

Introduction

At an early age, I realized that my desire for cooking was more than just a dream, it was a passion. My appetite began to grow as I learned many culinary secrets and mysteries working with a number of classically trained European chefs. The more experience I had in the inner sanctum of the professional kitchen, the more I developed my own brand of cooking techniques.

Cooking for me is an art, and René is my canvas. I am interested in every detail and color of the dining experience. I want to make it a memorable adventure for every guest. I love cooking. For so many reasons cooking is a joy! The heat from the fire. The comradery of my fellow cooks searing, grilling, dicing, mincing, deglazing, molding, frying, freezing, liquefying—and tasting, tasting, tasting.

The René at Tlaquepaque cookbook reveals my most closely guarded recipes. The cookbook is a collection of sweet and savory recipes that have been demystified, so even the novice cook can create memorable culinary delights. I've taken great care in every detail to insure that the recipes are easy to follow and that ingredients should be readily available at your local market.

I have found that making delicious food is the best way I can share the joy of dining together! When I arrive at René's in the morning I check the reservations to see if there are any large parties, important occasions, or special requests such as specific dietary needs or restrictions. Next I hold a brief meeting with the kitchen staff to go over the reservations. On to what I call my pre-flight check to insure all the equipment is functioning properly. Then into the dining room and patio to verify tables are properly set, silver shines, glassware sparkles, artwork is straight, and flowers are fresh. Back into the kitchen for quality control, tasting the soups, sauces, and dressings to insure they are up to René standards. Now it's time for what we call our "family meal," at which time I go over the daily specials with the staff, and we discuss guest's feedback. At last we are prepared and ready. The doors are unlocked, the curtain goes up, the show opens for another delightful day of dining.

I hope you too enjoy bringing people together at the table, creating a sense of community, sharing love, and delighting in making for guests and family a sensual experience of fine dining.

~Walter Paulson
Chef and Owner of René at Tlaquepaque

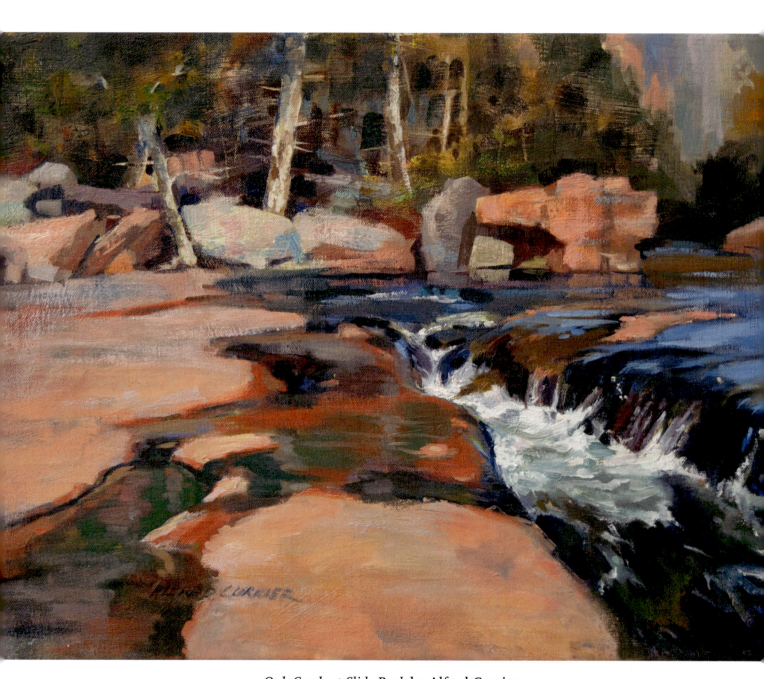

Oak Creek at Slide Rock by Alfred Currier

Acknowledgements

I am extremely proud of this project. A long and arduous journey, Sedona's *René at Tlaquepaque* has been ten years in the making. Only in the last year has the book finally begun to take shape—along with the challenging task of testing recipes, testing them over and over, shooting photos and sorting through hundreds of photos, editing, changing format and font. It has also been an emotional journey. Some days were easy and the excitement was overwhelming. Then there were other days that were not so easy and the fear was overwhelming. And I just wanted to give up.

This book has definitely been a team effort.

I would like to start at the beginning and acknowledge Gordon Heiss, owner of the Nantucket Lobster Trap, who taught me at an early age the old school European discipline of the professional kitchen.

To Marc Balloco, Director of Food and Beverage at L'Auberge de Sedona, who made me realize my true potential and to cook outside the box.

Most importantly I would like to give special thanks to my childhood friend Trudy Catterfeld for her expert guidance and tutelage. Without Trudy this book would be nothing more than a dream. Trudy you are as smart and articulate as you are beautiful.

Special thanks to Deborah Leatherwood for your support, encouragement, acute attention to detail, and your relentless pursuit of perfection. Thank you for your love and for putting up with me all these years.

Thanks to Vibhas Kendzia for his keen eye, attention to detail, and amazing photography. Vihbas, you've captured the essence of my culinary treasures. In addition, thanks to Kaisie Porter Wagner for your creativity.

I also want to thank the hundreds of friends that have supported and encouraged me over the years.

This book has been a labor of Love, not only for me but everyone involved in this project.

~Walter Paulson

Sedona, Arizona

Please come dine with us at René at Tlaquepaque when you visit Sedona—a land of magical red rock desert landscapes and beautiful twisted juniper trees. Only an hour and fifty minute drive from Phoenix, Sedona is located at the lower end of Arizona's spectacular Oak Creek Canyon, renowned for its stunning red buttes and monoliths and 5,000 to 7,000 foot high sandstone formations which appear to glow when illuminated by the rising or setting sun. The red rocks of Sedona are formed by a unique thick layer of red-to-orange colored sandstone rock known as the Schnebly Hill Formation.

The region's serene, magisterial nature inspires year-round activities, with miles of hiking and mountain biking trails. In just a single day you can enjoy lush river scenes, colorful desert foliage, vast red rock landscapes, and still have time to visit shops with traditional and contemporary art, and then complete your visit with a sumptuous meal at René at Tlaquepaque.

Here are only a few events that do change from year to year, but please consider when making a future reservation with us:

January	Sedona Chamber Music Festival
February	International Film Festival
March	Celebration of Spring—State Park Guided Tours
April	Sedona Studio Tour—Verde Valley Birding & Nature Festival
May	Cinco de Mayo Celebration at Tlaquepaque Arts & Craft Village
June	Illuminate Film Festival—Verde Valley Canyon Starlight Train Tour
July	Hopi Festival of Arts & Culture
August	Bike & Brew Festival—Sedona Arts Center Workshops
September	Mexican Independence Day at Fiesta del Tlaquepaque & Red Rocks Music Festival
October	Arts and Crafts Show—Hikes at the West Fork Trail in Oak Creek Canyon
November	Sedona Visual Arts Coalition Open Studio Tour
December	Festival of Lights at Tlaquepaque

Tlaquepaque

René at Tlaquepaque is nestled within the Tlaquepaque Arts and Crafts Village. Tlaquepaque (meaning the best of everything) is located on the banks of Oak Creek, modeled after its namesake in Guadalajara, Mexico. It is centrally located in Sedona and easily accessible on foot from local resorts or by trolley.

As you enter Tlaquepaque you will soak in the beautiful Sycamore trees, the lush gardens and the sparkling fountains. After exploring the many unique and wonderful galleries you can relax while enjoying a refreshing lunch or delightful dinner at René. Whether dining al fresco on the patio or inside with the windows open you can hear the soothing sounds of the water trickling from the fountains.

Tlaquepaque is where all your senses come alive!

Whatever the season Tlaquepaque is filled with music, art, recreation and life.

We look forward to seeing you and take you on a culinary journey!

Appetizers

Ahi Tartar

Dungeness Crab Cakes

Lobster Martini

Mushrooms Neptune

Smoked Salmon with Boursin Cheese Sauce on Roesti Potatoes

Southwestern Crab Cakes

Beef Carpaccio

Steak Tartar

Gruyere and Parmesan Beignets

Cheese Soufflé

Domaine Cheese

Sautéed Brie with Caramelized Apples

English Pea Griddle Cakes

Roasted Red Pepper Hummus

Ahi Tartar

Yields 4 servings

12 ounces finely diced ahi
4 tablespoons ahi dressing (recipe follows)
1 teaspoon finely diced red onion
2 tablespoons tomato concasse
1 teaspoon wasabi tobika
4 tablespoons chopped chives
8 tablespoons ponzu*
12 sesame seed tuiles**

In a small mixing bowl gently toss together the ahi, dressing, onion and tomato. Place a metal ring on the plate and fill with the ahi lightly packing it in. Place the caviar on top, sprinkle with the chives, drizzle the ponzu around the perimeter and serve with 3 tuiles.

Ponzu (yields 1 cup)
4 tablespoons lemon juice
½ cup rice vinegar
6 tablespoons soy sauce
2 tablespoons mirin
Zest of 1 lemon

In a small mixing bowl mix together all the ingredients

**Brush won ton wrappers with egg wash and sprinkle with sesame seeds then deep fry until golden brown.

Ahi Tartar Dressing (yields 1 cup)
½ cup lemon juice
3 tablespoons rice vinegar
¼ cup soy sauce
1 jalapeño seeded and minced
½ teaspoon grated ginger
½ teaspoon minced garlic
¼ cup sesame oil

Dungeness Crab Cakes

Yields 15 2-ounce portions

2 ounces butter
1 ½ ounces green bell pepper
1 ½ ounces button mushrooms
1 ½ ounces shallots
1 ½ ounces roasted red peppers
2 tablespoons flour
1 ½ cups half and half
2 teaspoons dry mustard
½ teaspoon salt
dash white pepper
1 tablespoon Worcestershire
1 pound Dungeness crab meat
1 ½ cups bread crumbs
hollandaise*

In the bowl of a food processor add the bell pepper, mushrooms, shallots and red pepper. Process until smooth. Melt the butter in a sauté pan. Add the pepper, mushroom, shallots and red pepper sauté until soft 5-10 minutes. Stir in the flour and cook 2 minutes. Add the ½ and ½, simmer the mixture 5 minutes then stir in the seasonings. Remove from heat and cool. When chilled add the crab meat and bread crumbs mix well. Portion into cakes. Heat a sauté pan with a little oil and add the cakes. Sauté 3–4 minutes per side. Remove from pan and top with hollandaise.

Hollandaise (yields 1 ¼ cups)
4 egg yolks
3 tablespoons water
8 ounces clarified butter
½ teaspoon Worcestershire
¼ teaspoon Tabasco
1 teaspoon lemon juice

Place egg yolks and water in a stainless steel mixing bowl. Place bowl over a pot of simmering water and begin whipping eggs with a wire whip, continue whipping until ribbons begin to form. Remove from heat and continue whipping while slowly adding the butter. When all the butter has been added, add the Worcestershire, Tabasco and lemon juice. Adjust seasoning to your personal taste.

Lobster Martini

Yields 4 servings

8 ounces fresh Maine lobster meat (2 1 ¼–pound lobsters steamed and chilled)
2 ruby red grapefruits
¼ cup red onion (diced)
½ jalapeño (seeded and diced)
3 tablespoons cilantro (chopped)
salt and pepper to taste

Peel the grapefruit, making sure to remove all the white pith and cut into membrane free segments. Toss the grapefruit segments with the onion, jalapeño and cilantro add salt and pepper to taste. Slice the lobster tail in half lengthwise. Spoon the grapefruit salsa into 4 chilled martini glasses. Arrange the tail meat over the salsa with 1 claw in each glass. Garnish with lemon twist and cilantro leaves.

Mushrooms Neptune

Yields 4 servings

24 button mushrooms
2 tablespoons butter
1 tablespoon chopped garlic
1 teaspoon chopped shallots
1 tablespoon cooking sherry
dash lemon juice
6 ounces cooked lobster meat
12 ounces cream cheese mixture (room temp)

Remove the stems from the mushrooms. Heat the butter in a sauté pan and add the garlic and shallots, sauté until translucent. Add the mushrooms and cook approximately 5 minutes until tender. Remove the mushrooms from the pan and set aside to cool. When cool place each mushroom upside down in each hole of an escargot dish or arrange on a plate next to each other so they will not tip over. Slice the lobster into 24 equal cubes and place each one inside the cavity where the stem once was. Cook in a 375 degree oven for 10 minutes until the mushroom and lobster are heated through. Spoon the cream cheese mixture in pastry bag or using a spoon put ½ ounce of cream cheese mixture over each mushroom. Return to the oven for an additional 2 minutes or until cheese is hot and begins to melt. Serve immediately.

Cream Cheese mix for Neptunes
¾ pound cream cheese (softened)
1 ½ teaspoons chopped shallots
¾ teaspoon chopped garlic
1 ½ teaspoons paprika

Cut cheese into 2 inch cubes. Put garlic and shallots in the food processor with cheese and paprika. Pulse continue pulsing until mixture is smooth, stopping to scrape down the sides. Be careful not to over mix

Smoked Salmon with Boursin Cheese Sauce on Roesti Potatoes

Yields 4 servings

16 ounces roesti potatoes*
8 ounces thinly sliced cold smoked salmon
8 ounces Boursin cheese sauce**
4 tablespoon chopped chives

Place a potato cake on each of four plates. Top with slices of salmon and spoon the sauce around the potato. Sprinkle with chives.

Roesti Potatoes (yields 4 4" round cakes)
Place whole unpeeled potatoes in a stock pot and add water to cover potatoes. Bring to a boil over high heat, cook for 15 minutes until al dente. Transfer potatoes to a plate and refrigerate until cool (1 hour). Peel and grate the potatoes. Heat a sauté pan, over medium heat, with a little butter and olive oil, using a 4" round ring mold pack the potatoes in about ¼" thick.

Season with salt and pepper. Cook 3–4 minutes until golden brown turn over and continue cooking an additional 3–4 minutes. When finished transfer to a plate and keep warm.

**Boursin Cheese Sauce (yields 1 cup or 4 servings)
1 tablespoon olive oil
1 tablespoon chopped shallots
¼ cup white wine
½ cup heavy cream
½ cup Boursin cheese
¼ cup chicken or vegetable stock
¼ teaspoon black pepper

Heat the oil in a sauce pan and sauté the shallots. Add the wine and stock simmer until reduced by half. Add the cream, cheese and pepper continue to simmer until sauce begins to thicken. Remove from heat and keep warm.

Southwestern Crab Cakes

Yields 15 2-ounce portions

2 ounces butter
1 ½ ounces roasted poblano chili
    roasted, peeled and seeded
1 ½ ounces button mushrooms
1 ½ ounces shallots
1 ½ ounces roasted red bell peppers
2 tablespoons flour
2 teaspoons chili powder
½ teaspoon cumin

2 teaspoons dry mustard
½ teaspoon salt
¼ teaspoon cayenne pepper
1 tablespoon Worcestershire
1 ½ cups half and half
1 ½ cups bread crumbs
1 pound blue crab meat
chipotle hollandaise*

Add the chili, mushrooms, shallots and red bell pepper in the bowl of a food processor. Begin processing until finely chopped. Melt butter in sauté pan and sauté vegetables until soft. Stir in flour to form a roux and cook for 2 minutes. Add cream and seasonings. Stir until smooth. Simmer for 5 minutes. Remove from heat and cool. When cool add crab meat (picked through for shells) and bread crumbs. Mix well and form into 2 ounce cakes. Heat a sauté pan with a little olive oil add the cakes, cook for 3–4 minutes per side until golden brown remove from pan and top with chipotle hollandaise. For the chipotle hollandaise stir chipotle powder into hollandaise to taste.

*Hollandaise (yields 1 ¼ cups)
4 egg yolks
3 tablespoons water
8 ounces clarified butter
½ teaspoon Worcestershire
¼ teaspoon Tabasco
1 teaspoon lemon juice
Add chipotle seasoning to taste

Place egg yolks and water in a stainless steel mixing bowl. Place bowl over a pot of simmering water and begin whipping eggs with a wire whip, continue whipping until ribbons begin to form. Remove from heat and continue whipping while slowly adding the butter. When all the butter has been added, add the Worcestershire, Tabasco and lemon juice. Add chipolte seasoning to your personal taste.

Beef Carpaccio

Yields 4 servings

12 ounces beef tenderloin, trimmed of all fat and sinew
3 tablespoons extra virgin olive oil
1 cup cilantro pesto*
½ cup shredded manchego cheese
toast points*

Place the meat in the freezer for about ten minutes. The meat should be very firm but not frozen. Using a very sharp knife slice the beef across the grain into paper thin slices. Divide the meat between four chilled plates spreading it out evenly over the surface of the plate. Sprinkle the meat with the olive oil and spoon the pesto over the meat and sprinkle with the cheese. Serve with toast points*.

*Slice a French roll into ¼ inch slices and spread out on a sheet pan. Place in a 375 degree oven for 4–6 minutes until golden brown.

*Cilantro pesto
⅓ cup macadamia nuts
1 tablespoon chopped garlic
2 tablespoons chopped shallots
1 cup cilantro (packed)
¼ cup feta cheese
½ cup olive oil

Spread out the nuts on a sheet pan and toast for 6 minutes at 375 degrees and let cool. Place the garlic, shallots, macadamia nuts, cilantro and cheese in the bowl of a food processor and process until thoroughly combined and smooth. Continue to process while slowly drizzling in the oil until everything is incorporated.

Steak Tartar

Yields 2 servings

6 ounces very lean beef tenderloin
1 clove garlic
2 anchovy filets
dash of salt
2 ounces yellow onion finely diced
15–20 capers
1 teaspoon Worcestershire

1 tablespoon olive oil
2 teaspoons ground black pepper
juice from ½ a lemon
¼ teaspoon tabasco
1 ½ tablespoon Dijon mustard
1 egg yolk

With a very sharp knife dice the meat very fine. Place the garlic in a mixing bowl and mash it using a dinner fork. Add the anchovies and salt continuing to mash everything together. Add the meat and work it into the garlic mixture with the fork. Add the onion and capers continuing to work it into the meat. Begin adding the remaining ingredients separately working it into the meat after each addition. After all the ingredients have been added form the meat into a patty and serve with cornichons and toast points.

Appetizers | 11

Gruyère and Parmesan Beignets

Yields 25 ½-ounce portions

2 ounces butter
½ cup water
½ cup flour
¾ cup grated Gruyère cheese
¾ cup grated parmesan cheese
2 whole eggs
½ teaspoon salt
Béarnaise sauce

In a saucepan bring the water and butter to a boil. Whisk in the flour. Transfer to the bowl of a kitchen aid. Add cheeses and salt mix on high speed until combined turn mixer down to low and add eggs one at a time mixing well after each addition. Refrigerate for 30 minutes. Meanwhile heat about two inches of oil in saucepan until it reaches 375 degrees. Scoop the batter with a #70 ice cream scoop* and carefully drop into hot oil and fry until golden brown. Serve with Béarnaise sauce.

*The number is based on how many scoops it takes to fill a 32-ounce container.

Hollandaise (yields 1 ¼ cups)
4 egg yolks
3 tablespoons water
8 ounces clarified butter
½ teaspoon worcestershire
¼ teaspoon tabasco
1 teaspoon lemon juice

Place egg yolks and water in a stainless steel mixing bowl. Place bowl over a pot of simmering water and begin whipping eggs with a wire whip, continue whipping until ribbons begin to form. Remove from heat and continue whipping while slowly adding the butter. When all the butter has been added, add the worcestershire, tabasco and lemon juice. Adjust seasoning to your personal taste.

Béarnaise
Add tarragon reduction to hollandaise. The amount depends upon your preference.

Tarragon Reduction
1 ½ tablespoons fresh tarragon leaves (finely chopped)
4 tablespoons red wine vinegar

Place tarragon and vinegar in sauté pan over low heat until all the liquid is gone. It will look like moist pipe tobacco. Let cool.

Cheese Soufflé

Yields 10 servings

3 tablespoons butter
3 tablespoons flour
1 cup milk
2+ tablespoons shredded parmesan cheese
½ cup grated Gruyère cheese
¼ teaspoon nutmeg
Salt and pepper to taste
4 eggs, separated

Preheat oven to 400 degrees. Melt butter in saucepan, stir in flour to form a roux. Add milk, simmer to thicken. Stir in cheeses, continue stirring until the cheese is melted and smooth, add spices. Remove from heat and set aside. Stir egg yolks into the béchamel. Place the egg whites in kitchen-aid and whip on high speed to form stiff peaks. Grease 10 3-ounce ramekins and coat with shredded parmesan. Spoon soufflé mixture into prepared ramekins. Bake for 20 minutes until puffed and browned. Serve immediately.

Domaine Cheese

Yields 1 quart

1 cup walnuts
12 ounces cream cheese
1 tablespoon chopped parsley
12 chives chopped
8 ounces Roquefort cheese

Place all the ingredients in the food processor and process until all the ingredients are thoroughly mixed and smooth, do not over mix. Serve with assorted crackers and raw vegetables.

Sautéed Brie with Caramelized Apples

Yields 4 servings

2 4-ounce wheels brie cheese
4 1 ½"-thick slices French bread
2 granny smith apples (peeled, cored and sliced)
4 tablespoons toasted almonds
1 tablespoon butter
1 tablespoon brown sugar
pinch cinnamon

Melt the butter in a sauté pan. Add the apples and begin to cook for 3–4 minutes. Add the sugar and cinnamon and cook for an additional 2–3 minutes until apples have a smooth coating of sugar if necessary add water and reduce until mixture is smooth and syrupy. Slice the wheels of brie in half-length wise and dust with flour. Heat a nonstick pan over medium heat add the brie rind side up and cook until brown, turn and finish until brie is heated throughout. While the cheese is cooking toast the bread. When the bread is toasted arrange on a plate, spoon apples over top with some liquid, place brie on top and finish with toasted almonds.

English Pea Griddle Cakes

Yields 1 quart or 12 2-ounce cakes

1 pound baby peas (fresh or frozen)
2 whole eggs + 2 yolks
1 cup heavy cream
6 tablespoons flour
6 tablespoons butter
½ teaspoon salt
¼ teaspoon white pepper
Mascarpone Cheese
tomato basil relish (recipe follows)

If using fresh peas, boil in salted water 5–10 minutes until tender. If using frozen place in boiling salted water until hot and tender. Whatever type of pea your using when done, strain and let cool. Place peas in the bowl of food processor with eggs and cream. Begin processing while

adding the flour. When the flour is fully incorporated stop processing. Add the salt and pepper. Brown the butter in a sauté pan. When browned add to the peas and continue processing until all the ingredients are incorporated and the mixture is smooth. To prepare, heat a nonstick Teflon pan, add 4–5 tablespoons batter and cook over medium high heat for 3 minutes or until the sides start to brown. Turn over and cook for another 2–3 minutes. Serve with mascarpone cheese and tomato basil relish. Garnish with whole basil leaves.

Tomato Basil Relish (yields 1 cup or 8 servings)
2 tomatoes (peeled, seeded and diced)
1 ½ teaspoons chopped garlic
8–10 large basil leaves (chiffonade)
2 tablespoons V-8 juice
Pinch salt and white pepper

In a small mixing bowl, mix together all the ingredients and chill.

Roasted Red Pepper Hummus

Yields 4 cups

1 cup garbanzo beans
1 yellow onion diced
1 clove garlic
1 bay leaf
salt and black pepper to taste

Soak beans overnight in water. Drain, rinse. Place beans in stock pot cover with water, bring to a boil and cook for 1 hour or until tender. Drain and cool.

2 cups cooked garbanzo beans
⅓ cup tahini
⅓ cup olive oil
4 cloves roasted garlic
2 cloves garlic

juice of 1 lemon
⅛ teaspoon cayenne
⅛ teaspoon cumin
⅛ teaspoon coriander
1 roasted red pepper

Place beans in food processor with the rest of the ingredients, puree, stopping occasionally to scrape the sides.

Soups

French Onion Soup Gratinee

Sweet Corn Soup with Smoked Chili Cream

Roasted Butternut Squash Soup with Fig Quenelle

Vegetarian Split Pea Soup

Lobster Bisque

Portobello Bisque

Tomato Bisque

Sweet Potato Bisque

Chilled Vichyssoise

Sweet Potato Vichyssoise

Chilled Gazpacho

Roasted Beet Gazpacho

French Onion Soup Gratinee

Yields 3 quarts or 12 8-ounce servings

2 ½ pounds medium yellow onions peeled and sliced
1 tablespoon olive oil
1 quart chicken stock
3 bay leaves
3 cloves
½ quart beef stock
3 ounces dehydrated onions
⅓ cup cooking sherry
½ cup dry red wine
1 tablespoon sugar
sliced French bread
olive oil
shredded Parmesan cheese
shredded Gruyère cheese
sliced Swiss cheese
sliced Provolone cheese

Heat oil in a stock pot. Add onions and cook over high heat until the onions begin to soften lower the heat and continue cooking adding the wine and sherry, until the onions are caramelized about 20 minutes. Add the stocks, bay leaf, cloves, dehydrated onions and sugar. Simmer for 1 hour.

To serve slice French bread ¼ inch thick spread out on a sheet pan, drizzle with olive oil and shredded parmesan cheese, toast in oven or under broiler until golden brown. Ladle soup into oven proof tureens. Float a crouton on top sprinkle with shredded Gruyère and place a slice of Swiss and provolone on top and brown under the broiler or in a 400 degree oven.

Sweet Corn Soup with Smoked Chili Cream

Yields 2 quarts

4 tablespoons butter
8 ounces yellow onion (finely diced)
2 teaspoons chopped garlic
4 ears (4 cups) sweet corn
¼ cup white wine

2 cups vegetable or chicken stock
½ teaspoon salt
¼ teaspoon ground black pepper
2 cups heavy cream
sugar to taste if needed

Melt butter in stock pot. Add onion and garlic, cook until soft. Add corn, cook letting corn absorb the butter. Add the wine and cook until the wine has reduced by half. Add stock, salt and pepper. Bring to a boil. Add cream, lower heat and simmer 10–15 minutes. Taste adding sugar if necessary. Remove from heat. Pour half the soup into a blender or food processor and puree, combine and serve with chopped cilantro and smoked chili cream.

Smoked Chili Cream

½ cup sour cream
1 teaspoon pureed canned chipotle chilies in adobo

½ teaspoon lime juice
salt and pepper to taste

Add all the ingredients in a mixing bowl and mix well.

Roasted Butternut Squash Soup with Fig Quenelle

Yields 1 ½ quarts or 6 8-ounce servings

3 tablespoons olive oil
2 ½ pounds butternut squash
6 ounces diced yellow onion
1 teaspoon chopped garlic
4 cups vegetable stock
2 teaspoon cinnamon
¼ teaspoon nutmeg

1 tablespoon peanut butter
1 ounce pure maple syrup
1 teaspoon salt
½ teaspoon black pepper
1 cup heavy cream
½ tablespoon sugar

Preheat oven to 375 degrees. Peel, seed and dice the squash. Place in a large mixing bowl and toss with 2 tablespoons olive oil. Spread out on a sheet pan and roast until tender 30–45 minutes. Heat 1 tablespoon olive oil in stock pot, add the onion and garlic, sweat. Add the squash, stock, and remaining ingredients, bring to a boil, lower heat and simmer for 30–45 minutes. Heat the cream and add to the soup. Puree using a stick blender or blender. Strain. Top with a fig quenelle.

Fig Quenelle
3 ½ ounces dried mission figs
2 tablespoons Myers's rum
1 cup heavy cream

Add all the ingredients to the food processor and process until smooth and creamy.

Vegetarian Split Pea Soup

Yields 3 quarts or 12 8-ounce servings

1 tablespoon olive oil
12 ounces carrots (peeled and diced)
6 ounces celery (diced)
8 ounces yellow onion (diced)
2 cups split peas (sorted and picked through)
2 ½ quarts water
3 teaspoons Worcestershire
1 teaspoon Tabasco
1 ½ teaspoons thyme
1 ½ teaspoons salt
¼ teaspoon white pepper

Heat the olive oil in a 4 quart stock pot. Add the vegetables and sauté until tender. Add split peas and water, bring to a boil. Lower heat to simmer, add spices and simmer for 1 ½ hours until peas are tender, you may have to add a little more water. Puree in a food processor or a blender, doing small amounts at a time. Serve with hot crusty French bread.

Lobster Bisque

Yields 1 ½ quarts

Lobster Stock

¼ cup olive oil
2 tablespoons butter
1–2 pounds lobster shells
1 onion peeled and chopped
1 carrot peeled and chopped
3 sticks celery chopped

⅛ teaspoon cayenne pepper
½ bunch parsley with stems
2 sprigs fresh tarragon
3 tablespoons tomato paste
½ cup dry white wine
2 tablespoons cognac

6 cups bottled clam juice
3 cloves garlic
1 teaspoon dry thyme
3 bay leaves
¼ teaspoon salt
⅛ teaspoon white pepper

Heat the oil and butter in a roasting pan. Add lobster shells and cook over medium heat for 15–20 minutes. Remove shells from roasting pan and place in stock pot. Deglaze roasting pan with cognac and add vegetables, cook for 10 minutes stirring occasionally scraping up the bits off the bottom of the pan. Two minutes before the vegetables are ready deglaze the pan with the wine. Add the vegetables to the pot with the shells, add remaining ingredients, except

salt and pepper. Place the stock pot over high heat, when stock comes to a boil reduce heat to a simmer. Occasionally skim the top. Simmer for 1 hour. Ten minutes before you remove the stock from the heat add the salt and pepper. When ready strain the stock discarding the shells and vegetables.

Lobster Bisque
1 ½ quarts lobster stock
½ cup roux*
½ cup heavy cream
1 tablespoon paprika
white truffle oil

In a large stock pot bring lobster stock to a boil. Reduce to a simmer and simmer for 30 minutes. Add the roux to thicken, cook for 10 minutes. Add the cream and paprika. Adjust seasonings to personal taste. Ladle into bowls and drizzle with truffle oil.

Roux
¼ pound butter
¾ cup flour

Melt the butter and stir in flour. Cook for 2 minutes until it begins to brown and emits a nutty aroma.

Portobello Bisque

Yields 2 ½ quarts or 10 servings

1 tablespoon olive oil
5 ounces chopped shallots
2 pounds portobello mushrooms
    (stemmed and chopped)
½ teaspoon thyme
¼ teaspoon salt
¼ teaspoon black pepper
¼ teaspoon grated nutmeg

¼ cup all purpose or gluten-free flour
⅓ cup sherry
1 ½ quarts mushroom stock
1 cup heavy cream
½ cup sour cream
white truffle oil
chopped chives

Heat the oil in a stock pot. Sweat the shallots. Add the mushrooms and cook until soft. Stir in the flour and cook for 3–5 minutes. Add the sherry, cook for another 3–5 minutes. Add the stock and seasonings, bring to a boil. Add the heavy cream and sour cream return to a boil, lower the heat and simmer for 15–20 minutes. Remove from heat puree and strain. Serve garnished with chopped chives and white truffle oil.

Tomato Bisque

Yields 1 ½ quarts or 6 8-ounce servings

3 pounds tomatoes (peeled with juice)*
12 ounces V-8 juice
8 ounces heavy cream
1 tablespoon oregano
1 ½ tablespoons basil
1 teaspoon salt
2 ½ teaspoons sugar
¼ teaspoon white pepper

Add tomatoes to stock pot with V-8 juice. Bring to a boil, reduce heat to a simmer, add spices and simmer for 30 minutes. Add heavy cream and simmer for 15 minutes. Remove from heat, puree in blender adding small amounts at a time. Serve hot in warm bowls. Garnish with whole basil leaves.

*peeling tomatoes
Core tomato, score an X on the bottom of the tomato. Place tomato in boiling water for 30 seconds or until the skin splits. Immediately transfer the tomato to a bowl of ice water. When they are cool enough to handle, peel off the skin with your fingers.

Sweet Potato Bisque

Yields 2 quarts or 8 8-ounce servings

1 tablespoon butter
1 tablespoon yellow onion (peeled and diced)
1 tablespoon celery (diced)
1 tablespoon carrot (peeled and diced)
½ jalapeño (seeded and diced)
4 cups chicken stock
2 cups heavy whipping cream
2 tablespoons maple syrup
½ teaspoon salt
¼ teaspoon black pepper
3 tablespoons lime juice
2 ounces pear brandy
2 pounds yams (cut into 1" cubes)
1 tablespoon sugar

Melt butter in a stock pot and sauté onions, celery, carrot, and jalapeño until soft. Add sweet potato, pear brandy, and chicken stock. Bring to a boil, reduce heat to simmer and cook until potatoes are tender, about 30–45 minutes. Add the remaining ingredients, bring back to a boil. Remove from heat, puree and strain. Serve hot in warm bowls. Garnish with sliced pear, avocado and lime.

Chilled Vichyssoise

Yields 1 quart or 4 8-ounce servings

1 ounce olive oil
6 ounces yellow onion
8 ounces leeks (white part only)
1 pound Yukon Gold Potatoes peeled and diced
2 cups chicken stock
1 cup heavy cream
1 cup milk
½ teaspoon salt
¼ teaspoon white pepper
1 tablespoon Dry Vermouth
chopped chives for garnish

Heat the olive oil in a 4 quart saucepan. Add the onion and sauté until the onion begins to caramelize, add the leeks and continue cooking until the leeks become tender. Add the potatoes and stock, cook 30–45 minutes until the potatoes are tender but not mushy. Remove from heat and puree. Heat the milk and cream. Return the potato puree to the pot and place on stove. Begin to simmer. Add the heated milk, cream, salt, pepper and vermouth. Adjust seasonings. Remove from heat and chill. Garnish with chopped chives.

Sweet Potato Vichyssoise

Yields 2 quarts or 8 8-ounce servings

1 tablespoon olive oil
4 ounces yellow onion (peeled and diced)
2 sticks celery (diced)
1 carrot (peeled and diced)
1 green bell pepper (seeded and chopped)
1 ¼ cups heavy whipping cream
½ teaspoon chopped garlic

1 pound yams (cut into 1" cubes)
1 quart water
1 ¼ cups orange juice
2 tablespoons honey
¼ teaspoon cayenne
1 teaspoon salt
spiced pecans*

Heat the oil in a large stock pot. Add onion, carrot, celery, bell pepper and garlic. Sauté until the veggies are soft. Add the orange juice and reduce by half. Add the sweet potatoes and water. Bring to a boil, reduce to a simmer and cook 30–45 minutes until the potatoes are tender (do not over cook the potatoes or they will taste watery). Add the honey, cayenne, and salt. Puree in a blender and strain pushing the solids through as much as possible. Return to heat

and add cream simmer for 10 minutes. Adjust the seasoning to taste. Remove from heat and chill. Serve in chilled bowls and garnish with spiced pecans.

Spiced Pecans (yields 1 ½ cups)
1 tablespoon butter
1 ½ cups pecans halves
¼ cup brown sugar
½ teaspoon paprika
1 teaspoon chili powder
1 ½ teaspoons cumin
3 tablespoons cider vinegar
2 tablespoons water

Melt the butter in a sauté pan. Add the pecans and cook for 3 minutes. Mix the spices with the sugar and add the sugar along with the water and cook until the sugar begins to caramelize. Add the vinegar and cook until most of the liquid has evaporated.

Chilled Gazpacho

Yields 2 quarts or 8 8-ounce servings

1 cucumber (peeled, seeded and diced)
1 green bell pepper (seeded and diced)
1 red bell pepper (seeded and diced)
1 cup celery (diced)
¼ cup green onions (sliced)
¼ cup white wine
¼ cup red wine vinegar

1 cup vegetable stock
1 cup V-8 juice
4 cups tomatoes (peeled, seeded and diced)
1 teaspoon salt
½ teaspoon fresh ground black pepper
dash tabasco

Place all the ingredients in a 3-quart container mix well, cover and refrigerate overnight. Serve in chilled bowls and garnish with corn tortilla chips.

Roasted Beet Gazpacho

Yields 2 quarts or 8 8-ounce servings

2 pounds tomatoes
    peeled, seeded and diced
1 red bell pepper
1 cucumber (peeled, seeded and diced
2 stalks celery chopped
1 tablespoon tomato paste
2 cups V-8 juice

2 ounces sherry vinegar
3 tablespoons sugar
1 tablespoon salt
½ teaspoon black pepper
½ tablespoon Durkee Red Hot sauce
1 pound roasted beets

Combine all the ingredients in a food processor and puree. Refrigerate.

Garnish

1 red bell pepper (seeded and diced)
1 yellow bell pepper (seeded and diced)
1 red onion (diced)
1 cucumber (peeled, seeded and diced)
1 red tomato (seeded and diced)
2 tablespoons chopped cilantro
1 teaspoon lime juice

Toss all the ingredients in mixing bowl and spoon over gazpacho.

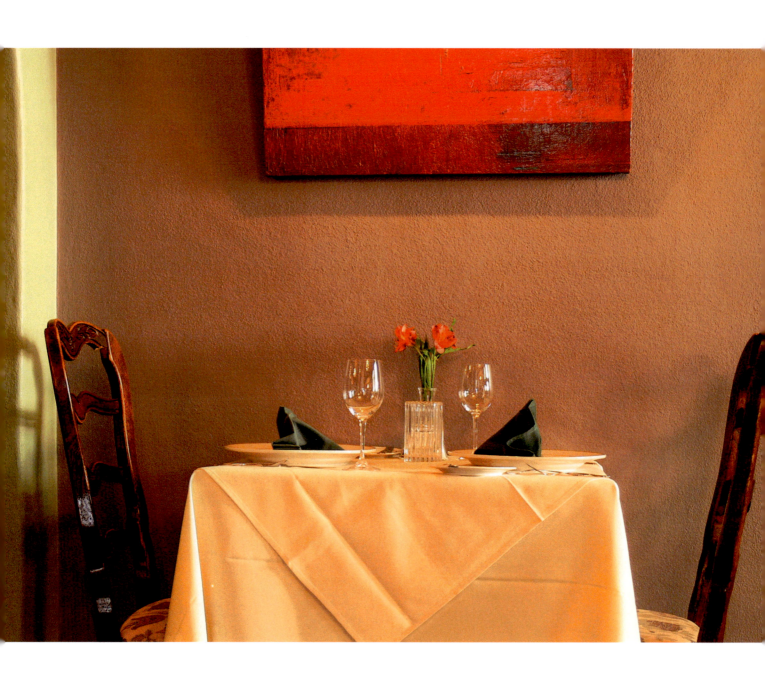

Salads

Arugula and Roasted Beet Salad

Kale and Quinoa Salad

Spinach and Tofu Salad

Spinach and Wild Mushroom Salad

Ahi Salad

Salmon Salad

Scallop Salad

Hearts of Romaine

Sautéed Miso Marinated Beef Salad

Arugula and Roasted Beet Salad

Yields 2 portions

4 cups loosely packed Arugula
1 ounce orange beet dressing*
16 slices roasted beets**
4 tablespoons crumbled goat cheese
2 tablespoons roasted, diced hazelnuts

Divide the arugula between 2 plates, spoon the dressing over the arugula. Garnish with the beets, goat cheese and hazelnuts.

Orange Beet Dressing (yields 1 cup)
4 ounces roasted beets**
4 ounces orange juice
¼ teaspoon chopped garlic

½ tablespoon fennel seed
1 ounce red wine vinegar
1 tablespoon lime juice
1 ½ ounces olive oil
salt and white pepper to taste

Dice roasted beets and add to a small saucepan with the orange juice, garlic and fennel. Bring to a boil, reduce heat to a simmer and reduce by half. Remove from heat and let cool. When cooled place in blender with vinegar and lime juice. Begin blending while slowly adding oil. Adjust seasonings.

**Roasted Beets
Wash beets and place in a roasting pan and fill half way up with water. Cover and cook for 2 hours at 400 degrees until tender. Remove from oven, uncover, let cool. Meanwhile measure 1 cup sugar and 1 cup rice vinegar in a sauce pan. Bring to a boil. Peel beets and add to vinegar mix. Reduce heat to a simmer. Simmer beets for 2 minutes per side. Remove from heat and let cool.

Kale and Quinoa Salad

Yields 4 portions

1 cup quinoa
2 cups chopped kale
1 cup shredded carrots
4 ounces roasted red beets
4 ounces roasted golden beets

4 tablespoons chopped tarragon
freshly ground black pepper
¼ cup olive oil
2 lemons, juiced
2 ounces toasted pine nuts

Add the quinoa to a sauce pot, add 2 cups salted water. Bring to a boil, reduce heat to a simmer and simmer for 3 minutes. Remove from heat, cover and let steam for 20 minutes until tender. Cool. Place the quinoa in a mixing bowl. Add the kale, tarragon, oil and lemon. Toss until all the ingredients are coated. Divide among 4 plates. Garnish with carrots, beets and pine nuts.

Spinach and Tofu Salad

Yields 2 servings

4 cups baby spinach (cleaned and trimmed)
1 ounce hazelnut vinaigrette
20 mandarin orange segments (fresh or canned)
20 sun-dried strawberries
4 ounces firm tofu
2 tablespoon peanut oil
1 teaspoon chopped garlic
2 teaspoons chopped shallots
2 tablespoons hazelnut oil
2 tablespoons soy sauce or Tamari
1 tablespoon water

Toss spinach leaves in a bowl with the vinaigrette. Arrange the spinach in the middle of two plates alternate the oranges and strawberries around the perimeter of the spinach. In a sauté pan heat the peanut oil add the garlic and shallots and slightly sauté. Add the tofu and hazelnut oil and the soy sauce cook for 2 minutes over high heat. Add the water and cook for 1 minute. Using a perforated spoon place the hot tofu over the spinach.

Hazelnut Vinaigrette (yields 1 ¾ cups)
⅓ cup sherry vinegar
½ teaspoon chopped garlic
¼ teaspoon black pepper
½ teaspoon Dijon mustard
1 egg yolk
1 ½ cups hazelnut oil

Place all the ingredients except the oil in the blender. Begin mixing while slowly adding oil.

Spinach and Wild Mushroom Salad

Yields 2 servings

4 cups spinach
1 ounce hazelnut vinaigrette
2 teaspoons chopped chervil
2 teaspoons chopped chives
3 ounces shitake mushrooms
2 tablespoons peanut oil
1 teaspoon chopped garlic
2 teaspoons chopped shallots
2 tablespoons hazelnut oil
2 tablespoons soy sauce or Tamari
2 tablespoons water

Toss the spinach leaves with the vinaigrette. Divide between two plates. Sprinkle chervil and chives over the spinach. In a sauté pan heat the peanut oil, add garlic, shallots, and mushrooms. Add hazelnut oil and cook until the mushrooms are tender. Add soy sauce and water. Serve mushrooms hot over spinach.

Hazelnut Vinaigrette (yields 1 ¾ cups)
⅓ cup sherry vinegar
½ teaspoon chopped garlic
¼ teaspoon black pepper
½ teaspoon Dijon mustard
1 egg yolk
1 ½ cups hazelnut oil

Place all the ingredients except the oil in the blender. Begin mixing while slowly adding oil.

Ahi Salad

Yields 4 servings

24 ounces sushi grade ahi tuna
6 ounces soy marinade*
4–12 inch flour tortilla
12 cups spring mix
2 ounces oriental citrus vinaigrette**
12 ounces cooked capellini
12 tomato slices
12 cucumber slices (scored)
8 tablespoons green onion (sliced)
8 tablespoons toasted macadamia nuts
4 tablespoons toasted black & white toasted sesame seeds
4 tablespoon pickled ginger
12 whole chives

Marinate the ahi in 3 ounces of the marinade for 30 minutes. Score the tortilla on a charcoal or gas grill and place on a 12-inch plate. Toss the greens with the citrus dressing, and arrange on tortilla, Toss the capellini with the remaining soy marinade, arrange on top of the greens. Arrange the tomato and cucumber slices around the salad. Sprinkle the green onions, macadamia nuts, sesame seeds and ginger over the entire salad. Sear the ahi until desired doneness is achieved and arrange around the salad. Garnish with the chives.

Soy Marinade (yields 1 cup)
½ cup soy sauce
¼ cup peanut oil
1 tablespoon mirin
¼ teaspoon sesame oil
¼ tablespoon minced cilantro
2 tablespoons thinly sliced green onions
1 tablespoon chopped garlic
1 tablespoon grated ginger
¼ teaspoon white pepper
1 tablespoon toasted sesame seeds
pinch dried red chili flakes

Place all the ingredients n in a mixing bowl and mix well with a wire whip.

****Oriental Citrus Vinaigrette (yields 1 ½ cups)***
1 cup orange juice
1 tablespoon toasted sesame seeds
1 tablespoon sugar
½ teaspoon salt
1 ½ tablespoons rice wine vinegar
1 tablespoon soy sauce
¼ cup peanut oil

Place all the ingredients except oil in a blender. Begin mixing while slowly adding oil.

Salmon Salad

Yields 2 servings

4 cups salad mix
8 red onion rings
24 mandarin orange segments
1 ounce orange basil vinaigrette*
2 4-ounce filets of salmon (¼" thick slices)
walnut pesto**

Toss the salad mix with the vinaigrette. Divide salad between two plates. Arrange the orange segments around the perimeter of the greens, place the onion rings over the top. Coat the salmon with the pesto and sauté 1 ½ minutes per side (or until desired doneness) arrange over greens.

*Orange Basil Vinaigrette (yields 1 ½ cups)
¼ cup balsamic vinegar
3 tablespoons red wine vinegar
½ teaspoon chopped garlic
¼ teaspoon black pepper
zest of ½ an orange
juice of 1 orange
3 basil leaves chopped
1 cup vegetable oil

Place all ingredients except oil in blender. Puree slowly while adding the oil in a steady stream. Blend until completely emulsified.

**Walnut Pesto
1 cup (2 ounces) basil
3 cloves garlic
¼ cup walnuts
¼ cup parmesan cheese
1 teaspoon red wine vinegar
3 ounces olive oil

Place all the ingredients except oil in food processor. Begin processing while slowly drizzling in the oil.

Scallop Salad

Yields 4 servings

12 sea scallops
8 cups mixed greens
16 slices Asian pear
1 ounce sesame vinaigrette
½ cup grated carrots
½ cup julienned daikon root
½ cup radish sprouts
black sesame seeds for garnish

Marinade
1 tablespoon Tamari
2 tablespoons sesame oil
1 teaspoon sesame seeds
sesame vinaigrette
1 teaspoon chopped garlic
2 teaspoons chopped ginger
1 ½ tablespoons Tamari
1 teaspoon Dijon mustard
½ teaspoon Sriracha sauce
½ cup seasoned rice vinegar
2 teaspoons honey
¾ cup sesame oil
¾ cup olive oil
1 teaspoon salt

Place scallops in a mixing bowl, add the marinade and marinate for 1 hour. For the vinaigrette, place all the ingredients except oils in a blender and begin blending while slowly adding the oils. Place the greens in a mixing bowl with the vinaigrette and toss until all the leaves are coated. Arrange on four plates. Arrange the pears, carrots, daikon and sprouts over lettuce. Sear the scallops until golden brown and done. Arrange over salad.

Hearts of Romaine

Yields 2 servings

4 cups romaine hearts
2 ounces + 1 tablespoon Dijon vinaigrette
2 ounces shredded manchego cheese
12 tomato petals*
36 French beans (blanched and marinated)**

In a large mixing bowl toss the romaine with the dressing and divide onto 2 chilled salad plates. Divide the cheese between the salads. Alternate 6 tomato petals and 18 beans over the top of the salad.

*Tomato Petals
Using a medium-sized tomato, core and slice into six wedges. Cut out the seeds and toss the petals in extra virgin olive oil and salt.

**French Beans
Blanch the beans, chill and toss with the 1 tablespoon dressing. Let stand for 10 minutes.

Variations
Marinate 2 6-ounce chicken breasts in 1 ounce vinaigrette for 20 minutes and cook on grill until done. Slice and arrange on top of salad.

Dijon Vinaigrette (yields 1 ½ cups)
¼ cup sherry vinegar
¼ cup balsamic vinegar
¼ cup Dijon mustard
2 tablespoons chopped shallot
¼ teaspoon salt
1/8 teaspoon ground black pepper
1 cup olive oil

Place all the ingredients except oil in a blender. Puree slowly while adding the oil in a steady stream.

Sautéed Miso Marinated Beef Salad

Yields 2 servings

12 ounces beef tenderloin (pounded thin)
4 tablespoons miso marinade*
8 cups loosely packed lettuce mix
2 ounces ginger mustard vinaigrette**
6 slices cucumber
6 red onion rings
12 blanched green beans

½ cup diced tomatoes
2 cups carrot strings
½ cup roasted peanuts
2 tablespoons chopped chives
2 tablespoons chopped cilantro
8 sesame tuiles***

Marinate the beef in the marinade. In a mixing bowl toss the lettuce with the dressing, divide among 2 large salad plates. Arrange the remaining vegetables on top of the greens. Sprinkle with the peanuts, chives and cilantro. Heat a nonstick sauté pan and sear the beef for 1 minute on each side. Arrange the beef on top of the salad.

Miso Marinade
2 tablespoons red miso
5 tablespoons sugar
1 teaspoon grated fresh ginger
½ teaspoon garlic

2 tablespoons sesame oil
1 teaspoon soy sauce
2 tablespoons mirin

In a small mixing bowl add all the ingredients and mix well.

Ginger Mustard Vinaigrette (yields 1 cup)
3 teaspoons grated ginger
1 teaspoon chopped garlic
½ cup rice vinegar
2 tablespoons soy sauce
2 tablespoons brown sugar

pinch crushed red pepper
4 teaspoons Dijon mustard
3 teaspoons sesame oil
2 tablespoons peanut oil

Combine the ginger, garlic, vinegar, soy sauce, sugar, pepper and mustard in a blender let sit for 20 minutes at room temperature to let the flavors combine. Begin blending on high speed and slowly drizzle in the oils.

Sesame Tuiles (yields 8)
2 tablespoons sesame seeds
¼ teaspoon sugar

pinch salt & cayenne
1 egg white
2 teaspoons corn starch
8 won ton wrappers

Mix together sesame seeds, sugar, salt and cayenne. Add corn starch to egg white and whip until corn starch is dissolved. Brush egg white on won ton wrappers and sprinkle with sesame seed mixture. Arrange on a sheet pan and cook at 400 degrees until golden brown.

Entrees

Champagne Veal

Fettuccini Bolognese

Madame Oak Creek

Chicken Crepes

Chicken Piccata

Southwestern Chicken Cordon Bleu

Chicken Marsala

Eggs Benedict

Eggs Florentine

Braised Lamb Shank

Roasted Pork Tenderloin with Sun-Dried Cherry Sauce and Creamed Pine Nuts

Tenderloin of Beef with Whisky Juniper Berry Sauce

Cedar Plank Salmon with Roasted Red Pepper Salsa

Rocky Mountain Rainbow Trout Almondine

Sauté Sand Dabs au Meunière

Acorn Squash

Eggplant Parmesan

Wild Mushroom Strudel

Portobello Bolognese

Seitan Wellington

Spaghetti Squash Primavera

Tournedos Au Poivre

Champagne Veal

Yields 2 servings

2 tablespoons olive oil
flour as needed
8 ounces veal tenderloin
3 ounces shitake mushrooms
    stemmed and sliced
1 sprig fresh thyme

1 bay leaf
3 ounces champagne
3 ounces demi-glace
1 ounce tomato concasse
3 ounces whole butter (room temp)
2 tablespoons chopped chives

Trim and slice the veal into 4 portions place veal between two pieces of plastic wrap and with a meat mallet pound out to about ⅛ of an inch. Heat the oil in a large sauté pan. Dust the veal with flour and add to the pan. Brown the veal on one side about one minute. Turn the veal add the thyme, bay leaf, mushrooms and champagne. Reduce by half. Add the demi-glace and reduce until the sauce coats the back of a spoon. Remove the veal and divide between 2 dinner plates. Add the tomato to the sauce and stir in the butter. Spoon the sauce over the veal and sprinkle with chives.

Fettuccine Bolognese

Yields 8 8-ounce portions

2 tablespoons olive oil
2 pounds ground beef or veal
½ pound sweet Italian sausage
1 ½ cups (6 ounces) diced yellow onions
½ cup (6 ounces) diced carrots
1 tablespoon chopped garlic
1 cup cabernet
4 cups ground pear tomatoes
1 tablespoon dried basil

1 teaspoon dried thyme
½ teaspoon dried oregano
1 bay leaf
1 tablespoon beef base
1 tablespoon sugar
1 teaspoon salt
½ teaspoon black pepper
fettuccine

Heat the oil over moderate heat in a large stock pot. Add the onions and cook until it begins to brown add a little water and continue cooking until onions have caramelized. Add the carrots and garlic. Continue to cook until the carrots are tender crisp. Add the meat and sausage and cook stirring occasionally. Continue cooking until the meat is thoroughly cooked and no longer pink. Add the remaining ingredients and simmer for 1 ½ hours. Check seasonings. Toss with pasta.

Madame Oak Creek

Yields 2 servings

8 ounces veal scallopini
4 ounces sliced mushrooms
8 ounces madame oak creek sauce*
1 tablespoon olive oil

Heat the oil in sauté pan. Dust the veal with flour. Place the veal in a sauté pan with hot oil cook for 45 seconds turn add mushrooms and sauce, reduce.

Madame Oak Creek Sauce (yields 8 cups)

6 cups demi-glace
6 ounces au-jus
8 ounces red wine
1 ½ ounce Maggi seasonings
¾ ounce Worcestershire
4 ounces madeira
4 tablespoons corn starch

In a large stock pot bring the demi-glace to a boil. Add the au-jus, red wine, Maggi and Worcestershire. In a small mixing bowl combine the madeira and cornstarch. Mix well to form a slurry, add to the stock. Bring back to a boil reduce heat to a simmer and simmer for 20 minutes. Remove from heat. Strain. Place in freezer, the fat will float to the top and harden. When hardened skim off the fat. The stock will keep refrigerated for 1 week or frozen up to 6 months.

Chicken Crepes

Yields 10 4-ounce crepes

1 pound boneless, skinless chicken breasts
2 ½ cups chicken stock
2 bay leaves
4 whole cloves
½ teaspoon salt
¼ teaspoon white pepper

4 ounces button mushrooms, sliced
1 cup heavy cream
½ teaspoon salt
¼ teaspoon white pepper
roux*

Add the chicken and stock to a 3 quart saucepan. Bring to a boil, reduce heat to medium, cook 10–12 minutes or until chicken is done. Remove the chicken from the stock and let cool. Meanwhile heat the cream over medium heat. Dice the chicken when it is cool enough to handle. Add the chicken, mushrooms, cream, salt and pepper to the stock. Bring to a simmer over medium heat. Turn the heat down to low. Stir in the roux a little at a time, cooking it for 3–5 minutes after each addition, until the desired consistency is achieved (it should be very thick).

*Roux
4 ounces butter
¾ cup flour

Melt the butter in a sauté pan. Whisk in the flour and cook for 2 minutes.

Crepes (yields 12 crepes)
3 eggs
1 ¼ cups milk
2 tablespoons melted butter
¼ cup + 2 tablespoons flour
½ teaspoon salt

Place all the ingredients into a mixing bowl. Mix together with a wire whip until smooth. Let rest refrigerated for 30 minutes. Heat a crepe pan or an 8 inch nonstick Teflon coated sauté pan with a little butter. Spoon enough batter into pan to just cover the bottom and swirl pan so batter is evenly distributed. Cook over low to medium heat until bubbles appear around the edges. Flip crepe over and cook 1 ½ to 2 minutes on the other side. Remove from the pan and let cool at room temperature. The crepes can be used immediately or stored in the refrigerator for 4–5 days or frozen for up to a month.

Hollandaise (yields 1 ¼ cups)
4 egg yolks
3 tablespoons water
8 ounces clarified butter
½ teaspoon Worcestershire
¼ teaspoon tabasco
1 teaspoon lemon juice

Place egg yolks and water in a stainless steel mixing bowl. Place bowl over a pot of simmering water and begin whipping eggs with a wire whip, continue whipping until ribbons begin to form. Remove from heat and continue whipping while slowly adding the butter. When all the butter has been added, add the Worcestershire, Tabasco and lemon juice. Adjust seasoning to your personal taste.

Béarnaise
Add tarragon reduction to hollandaise. The amount depends upon your preference.

Tarragon Reduction
1 ½ tablespoons fresh tarragon leaves (finely chopped)
4 tablespoons red wine vinegar

Place tarragon and vinegar in sauté pan over low heat until all the liquid is gone. It will look like moist pipe tobacco. Let cool.

56 | Entrees

Chicken Piccata

Yields 4 servings

4 6-ounce boneless, skinless chicken breasts
flour to dust
2 tablespoons olive oil
2 tablespoons capers
2 ounces lemon juice
3 ounces demi-glace
2 tablespoons whole butter

Heat the oil in a sauté pan. Dust the chicken with flour and place in heated pan brown on one side 3–4 minutes and turn, add lemon juice and capers, lower heat and reduce slightly, add demi-glace and continue to cook over low heat until chicken is cooked and sauce is thick enough to coat the back of a spoon. Remove from heat and stir in the butter.

Southwestern Chicken Cordon Bleu

Yields 4 servings

4 6-ounce boneless, skinless chicken breasts
8 ounces thinly sliced ham
6 ounces grated asiago cheese
4 roasted, peeled, seeded Anaheim chilies
6 ounces roasted red pepper cream

Place the chicken between 2 pieces of plastic wrap and pound out to ⅛ inch. Arrange 2 ounces of ham, 1 ½ ounces of cheese and 1 chili over each chicken breast. Roll up very tightly. Preheat oven to 400 degrees. Place chicken seam side down in a greased baking dish and cook for 12 minutes or until cooked through. Divide the sauce between 4 plates. Slice chicken and arrange over sauce.

Roast Red Pepper Cream (yields 2 cups)

3 cloves garlic
2 shallots sliced
2 sticks celery chopped
2 cups white wine

1 cup heavy cream
1 pound butter cut into 1 inch cubes
3 roasted red peppers finely chopped

Add vegetables with garlic and shallots to wine. Simmer until reduced by half. Add heavy cream and reduce by half. Remove from heat and whip in butter a little at a time. Add salt & white pepper to taste. Strain.

Chicken Marsala

Yields 4 servings

2 tablespoons olive oil
4 6-ounce chicken breasts
4 ounces sliced wild mushrooms
3 ounces marsala
6 ounces demi-glace
6 ounces heavy cream

Heat the oil in a sauté pan over medium heat. Dust the chicken breast with flour and place in pan and brown on one side turn over and continue cooking. Add the mushrooms and marsala. Reduce by half. Add demi-glace, reduce, slowly add heavy cream and reduce.

Eggs Benedict

Yields 2 servings

4 eggs
2 English muffins
4 1 ½ ounce slices Canadian bacon
8 tablespoons hollandaise

In a large shallow saucepan bring a mixture of water and white vinegar to a boil. (One quart water to 1 tablespoon vinegar). Meanwhile split the English muffin, toast and butter. Keep warm. Sauté the Canadian bacon and place each slice on top of each muffin. Meanwhile add the whole eggs to the boiling water, cover and turn off the heat. Cook for 3 ½ minutes. Remove the eggs carefully with a slotted spoon or skimmer and place over bacon. Spoon 2 tablespoons hollandaise over each egg and serve.

Hash Browns (yields 4 servings)
1 pound Yukon gold potatoes
butter
olive oil
salt
pepper

Par cook the potatoes until they are slightly underdone. Cool and store in refrigerator until ready to use. Peel and coarsely grate the potatoes. Heat a sauté pan and add a small amount of butter and olive oil. Place the potatoes in the heated pan and season with salt and pepper. Cook the potatoes until they are golden brown. Turn and cook the other side until golden brown and heated through.

Hollandaise (yields 1 ¼ cups)

4 egg yolks
3 tablespoons water
8 ounces clarified butter

½ teaspoon Worcestershire
¼ teaspoon tabasco
1 teaspoon lemon juice

Place egg yolks and water in a stainless steel mixing bowl. Place bowl over a pot of simmering water and begin whipping eggs with a wire whip, continue whipping until ribbons begin to form. Remove from heat and continue whipping while slowly adding the butter. When all the butter has been added, add the Worcestershire, Tabasco and lemon juice. Adjust seasoning to your personal taste.

Eggs Florentine

Yields 2 servings

4 eggs
2 English muffins
spinach mixture*
8 tablespoons hollandaise

In a large shallow saucepan bring a mixture of water and white vinegar to a boil. (1 quart water to 1 tablespoon vinegar). Meanwhile split the English muffin, toast and butter. Keep warm. Meanwhile add the whole eggs to the boiling water, cover and turn off the heat cook for 3 ½ minutes. Spoon the spinach mixture over the muffins using a slotted spoon or skimmer remove the eggs from the water and place over the spinach. Spoon 2 tablespoons hollandaise over each egg and serve.

Spinach mixture
Heat a sauté pan with 1 teaspoon of olive oil, add 1 teaspoon chopped garlic and 1 teaspoon chopped shallots. Cook until soft add 8 ounces spinach leaves cook until wilted. Add 3 ounces heavy cream and reduce until most of cream has evaporated.

ature *Hash Browns (yields 4 servings)*
1 pound Yukon gold potatoes
butter
olive oil
salt
pepper

Par cook the potatoes until they are slightly underdone. Cool and store in refrigerator until ready to use. Peel and coarsely grate the potatoes. Heat a sauté pan and add a small amount of butter and olive oil. Place the potatoes in the heated pan and season with salt and pepper. Cook the potatoes until they are golden brown. Turn and cook the other side until golden brown and heated through.

Hollandaise (yields 1 ¼ cups)
4 egg yolks
3 tablespoons water
8 ounces clarified butter
½ teaspoon Worcestershire

¼ teaspoon Tabasco
1 teaspoon lemon juice

Place egg yolks and water in a stainless steel mixing bowl. Place bowl over a pot of simmering water and begin whipping eggs with a wire whip, continue whipping until ribbons begin to form. Remove from heat and continue whipping while slowly adding the butter. When all the butter has been added, add the Worcestershire, Tabasco and lemon juice. Adjust seasoning to your personal taste.

Braised Lamb Shank

Yields 4 servings

4 tablespoons olive oil
4 lamb fore shanks
mire poix (2 onions, 6 carrots, ½ stalk celery, 1 ounce garlic, chopped and diced)
1 quart cabernet
46 ounces V-8 juice
2 quarts demi-glace
6 bay leaves
1 ½ teaspoons whole cloves
2 tablespoons thyme
1 tablespoon oregano
2 tablespoons sage
1 tablespoon cumin
2 tablespoons basil

Heat the oil in a large roasting pan, add the shanks and sear on all sides. Remove the shanks and set aside. Add the mire poix and sweat. Deglaze the pan with the wine and add the shanks back to the pan. Add the V-8, demi-glace, and herbs. Bring to a boil. Remove from heat, cover, and place in a 375 degree oven and bake for 3 ½ hours. Remove the shanks from the sauce and strain the sauce. Place the shanks on plates and ladle the sauce over the shanks.

Roasted Pork Tenderloin with Sun-Dried Cherry Sauce and Creamed Pine Nuts

Yields 2 servings

2 tablespoons olive oil
2 6–7 ounce pork tenderloin
1 ½ tablespoons garlic (chopped)
½ teaspoon chopped shallots
2 ounces sun-dried Bing cherries
1 cup cabernet sauvignon
1 cup port
4 ounces demi-glace
2 ounces whole butter (room temp)
3 ounces heavy cream
2 tablespoons pine nuts (toasted)
2 tablespoons blue cheese

Pre heat the oven to 375 degrees. Heat the oil in a medium saucepan. Add the pork to the pan. Sear the pork on all sides and remove from the pan, place on a baking sheet and place in the oven until cooked to desired temperature 9–10 minutes for medium well. When done remove from oven and keep warm. Meanwhile add garlic, shallots and cherries to sauce pan and sauté 2–3 minutes. Deglaze the pan with the cabernet and reduce by ⅔. Add the port and reduce by ⅔. Add the demi-glace, reduce by ½, remove from heat and stir in the butter. While the wines are reducing, in a small saucepan add the cream, cheese and nuts. Reduce over a medium low flame until slightly thickened. When the pork is cooked and both sauces are ready. Spoon ½ the cherry sauce onto 2 plates. Slice the pork and arrange over the sauce. Spoon the creamed pine nuts over the pork.

Tenderloin of Beef with Whisky Juniper Berry Sauce

Yields 2 servings

1 tablespoon olive oil
10 ounces beef tenderloin
1 teaspoon chopped garlic
1 tablespoon chopped shallots
1 tablespoon juniper berries
2 ounces scotch

2 ounces gin
2 ounces demi-glace
1 teaspoon chopped tarragon and mint
1 teaspoon whole grain mustard
1 teaspoon red currant jelly
1 tablespoon whole butter (room temperature)

Heat olive oil in a sauté pan. Sear beef in hot oil. Remove beef from pan and keep warm. Add garlic, shallots and juniper berries to sauté pan and heat over medium heat until translucent. Remove pan from heat, add scotch and return to heat (pan should flame). When flame dies, remove pan from heat, add gin, return to heat, (flame again) and reduce. Strain liquid and return to heat. Add demi-glace, tarragon, mint, currant jelly, and mustard. Reduce once more. Bring the beef up to desired temperature under the broiler. Slowly stir the butter into the sauce. Spoon onto plates, slice the beef and arrange over sauce.

Cedar Plank Salmon with Roasted Red Pepper Salsa

Yields 2 servings

2 7–8 ounce salmon filet
6 ounces roasted red pepper salsa*

Preheat oven to 400 degrees. Place the salmon on a cedar plank and rub the salmon with olive oil. Place in the oven and cook for 10 minutes per inch of thickness. When done the salmon should flake easily. When done transfer to plates and spoon salsa over salmon.

Roasted red pepper salsa (yields 4 servings)
2 large red bell peppers (roasted, peeled, seeded and chopped)
¼ cup Greek or nicoise olives (pitted and chopped)
⅓ cup parmesan cheese
¼ cup olive oil
2 tablespoons fresh lime juice
1 bunch green onions
3 tablespoons chopped cilantro
salt and black pepper to taste

Place all the ingredients in a mixing bowl and toss together. Let sit in the refrigerator for at least 2 hours or overnight to let the flavors develop.

Rocky Mountain Rainbow Trout Almondine

Yields 1 trout

1 8-ounce boneless rainbow trout
1 ounce sliced toasted almonds
1 tablespoon whole butter
1 lemon wrap

Dust the trout with flour and sauté. Cook flesh side down for 2 minutes, turn and cook an additional 2 minutes. Brown butter in sauté pan. Place the trout in the center of the plate; sprinkle with almonds, pour butter over fish.

Sautéed Sand Dabs au Meunière

Yields 2 servings

2 tablespoons olive oil
12 ounces sand dabs (boned and skinned)
flour as needed
2 teaspoons lemon juice
2 teaspoons browned butter

In a large sauté pan heat the olive oil. Dust the filets with flour and add to the hot pan. Cook for 30–45 seconds on each side. Remove from pan and divide between 2 plates. Add the butter to a small hot sauté pan and cook over low heat until the foam subsides and butter begins to brown and emit a nutty aroma. Squeeze lemon juice over the fish and pour butter over the fish.

Acorn Squash

Yields 6 servings

3 acorn squash
melted butter for brushing squash
1 ounce olive oil
12 ounces yellow onion (diced)
1 tablespoon chopped garlic
1 red bell pepper (seeded and diced)
1 green bell pepper (seeded and diced)
1 yellow bell pepper (seeded and diced)
12 ounces cremini mushrooms (chopped)
4 ounces red cabbage (chopped)
½ ounce amaretto plus some for sprinkling
6 ounces goat cheese
6 ounces chopped macadamia nuts
salt and pepper

Preheat oven to 400 degrees. Cut the squash in half and remove seeds. Brush flesh with butter and sprinkle with amaretto. Place squash on sheet pan flesh side up. Roast in oven for 20–30 minutes until tender but firm. Heat oil in a sauté pan. Add onions and garlic sauté for 2 minutes, add peppers cook 2 more minutes, add mushrooms, cabbage, amaretto, salt and pepper. Cook until tender. Remove from heat and mix in cheese and nuts. Spoon mixture into squash halves.

Eggplant Parmesan

Yields 4 servings

1 medium to large eggplant
egg wash*
2 cups bread crumbs
2 cups shredded parmesan
1 teaspoon salt
1 teaspoon black pepper

1 teaspoon granulated garlic
2 teaspoons each dried oregano and basil
2 tablespoons olive oil
creamy tomato sauce**
mozzarella
fresh basil chiffonade

In the bowl of a food processor add the bread crumbs, parmesan cheese, spices and herbs and process until you achieve a fine texture. Peel the eggplant and slice into half inch slices. Dip eggplant slices in egg wash and coat with bread crumb mixture. Heat the olive oil in a sauté pan, add the eggplant slices and sauté over medium heat for 3 minutes turn over and cook for an additional 3 minutes. Transfer to a baking sheet pan and top with mozzarella slices. Place under broiler until cheese begins to melt. Meanwhile heat the tomato sauce and ladle sauce onto plates, place eggplant over sauce and garnish with basil.

***Egg Wash**
6 whole eggs
3 tablespoons water

Crack the eggs into a blender, add the water and blend until the eggs are thoroughly whipped.

****Creamy Tomato Sauce**
1 tablespoon olive oil
1 tablespoon chopped garlic
1 tablespoon shallots
2 cups diced tomatoes (peeled and seeded)
½ teaspoon salt
1 ½ teaspoons sugar
3 ounces cream cheese

Heat oil in a saucepan. Add shallots and garlic, sweat. Add tomatoes, salt and sugar. Bring to a boil, reduce heat to a simmer, simmer for 5 minutes. Add cheese and stir until incorporated. Remove from heat and puree.

Wild Mushroom Strudel

Yields 12 servings

¼ cup olive Oil
8 ounces diced yellow onion
2 teaspoons chopped garlic
½ teaspoon dried thyme
½ teaspoon salt
1 teaspoon black pepper

2 pounds assorted mushrooms (sliced)
1 cup crumbled feta cheese
1 cup shredded provolone
1 sheet puff pastry thawed
egg wash*

Heat olive oil in large soup pot. Add the onion and garlic, sauté until soft. Add the mushrooms, salt, pepper and thyme cook until all the juices have evaporated. Cool in the refrigerator. When cool mix in the cheeses. Lay out the puff pastry, brush the edges with egg wash. Spread the mushroom mixture over the lower ⅓ of the Pastry, form into a log shape, Bring the bottom end of the pastry up, and roll to seal. Seal all the edges. Brush entire pastry with egg wash. Bake at 375 for 20 minutes until golden brown. Let rest 15 minutes before slicing.

***Egg Wash*
1 egg
1 tablespoon water

Crack egg into mixing bowl, add water and whip well with wire whip.

Portobello Bolognese

Yields 4 8-ounce servings

2 tablespoons olive oil
2 teaspoons chopped garlic
8 ounces grated yellow onion
4 ounces grated carrots
4 ounces celery (finely diced)
1 teaspoon salt
½ teaspoon black pepper
½ teaspoon thyme
2 teaspoons basil
20 ounces portobellos (stemmed and chopped)
3 tablespoons tomato paste
1 cup vegetable stock
½ cup red wine
1 ounce rehydrated porcini mushrooms
½ tablespoon sugar

Heat the oil in a saucepan. Add garlic, onion, carrot and celery sauté until tender. Add seasonings and portobellos. Cook over low heat 15–20 minutes. Add remaining ingredients. Simmer for 20 minutes. To serve ladle over spaghetti squash or pasta of choice.

Seitan Wellington

Yields 4 servings

6 ounces seitan mix
⅛ teaspoon ginger powder
dash cayenne
1 teaspoon chopped garlic

2 tablespoons soy sauce
1 ½ teaspoons Maggi seasoning
¾ cup water

Mix together dry ingredients and wet ingredients separately. In a stainless steel mixing bowl add the wet and the dry ingredients. Mix well and knead for 5 minutes. Divide the seitan into 8 equal balls, and form into small patties. Dust each patty with flour. Heat the olive oil in a sauté pan and sauté the seitan for 2 minutes per side (or until golden brown on both sides). Remove from pan and let drain on paper towels. Refrigerate until ready to use or wrap tightly with plastic wrap and freeze

Mushroom Duxelles (yields ½ cup)

¼ cup yellow onions
½ cup button mushrooms
2 teaspoons chopped shallots
1 teaspoon chopped garlic

1 tablespoon soy sauce
2 tablespoons chopped walnuts
1 tablespoon peanut oil

In the bowl of a food processor chop the onion, shallot, garlic and walnuts separately. Heat the oil in a sauté pan, add the garlic, shallots and onion. Sauté 5 minutes until tender. Finely chop the mushrooms add to the pan along with the soy sauce and walnuts. Cook over medium heat until all the liquid has evaporated

Herb Pesto (yields ½ cup)

¾ cup basil, packed
½ cup cilantro, packed
3 tablespoons chervil, packed
1 teaspoon chopped garlic

¼ cup olive oil
¼ cup toasted pine nuts*
salt and pepper to taste

Place all the ingredients except oil in a food processor, begin processing while slowly drizzling in the oil. Add salt & pepper to taste.

*To toast the pine nuts lay them out evenly on a sheet pan and place in a 375 oven for 10 minutes. Let cool before using in the pesto.

Seitan (assembly)
1 sheet puff pastry
4 tablespoons mushroom duxelles
8 tablespoons herb pesto
8 seitan rounds
8 ¼" firm tofu rounds
egg wash**

Sprinkle flour on your cutting board, place your puff pastry on the floured cutting board and sprinkle more flour on the pastry. With a rolling pin roll out the pastry to 1/8 inch thickness. Cut four 7 inch by 7 inch squares out of the pastry. Slice the tofu into ¼ inch thick squares and with a 2 ¾ inch cookie cutter cut 8 rounds(reserve trimmings for bordelaise sauce). To assemble on each pastry sheet place 1 tablespoon mushroom duxelles, in the center, top with a tofu round, 1 tablespoon pesto, seitan round, tofu round, 1 tablespoon pesto, and seitan round. Brush the edges with the egg wash and wrap the pastry around sealing all edges. Brush the entire outside of the pastry with egg wash. Repeat with the other three. Preheat oven to 400 degrees. Bake for 20 minutes. Serve with the bordelaise sauce.

**Egg Wash
2 whole eggs
1 tablespoon water

Whip ingredients together.

Vegetarian Espagnole Sauce (yields 2 ¾ cups)
1 tablespoon olive oil
½ yellow onion, rough chopped
1 carrot, rough chopped
4 ounces button mushrooms
2 sticks celery
½ tablespoon shallots chopped
½ teaspoon chopped garlic
1 cup red wine
3 tablespoons red miso
2 sprigs thyme
2 bay leaves
1 sprig rosemary
2 whole cloves
3 black peppercorns
2 tablespoons soy sauce
3 cups water
2 tablespoons tomato paste

Heat the oil in a stock pot. Add the vegetables and sauté until tender about 15 minutes. Deglaze pan with red wine and reduce by half approximately about 15 minutes. Add the remaining ingredients. Bring to a boil. Reduce heat to a simmer. Simmer for 1 hour. Remove from heat strain and let cool. Use this sauce to make the bordelaise. Any sauce left over should be poured into ice cube trays and freeze.

Vegetarian Bordelaise (yields 4)
1 cup espagnole sauce
3 teaspoons chopped shallots
⅛ teaspoon ground black pepper
1 thyme sprig
3 tablespoons finely diced tofu

Briefly sauté the shallots in a sauté pan. Add the espagnole sauce, pepper and thyme. Cook over medium heat for 10 minutes. Remove thyme and add the tofu and cook an additional 2 minutes.

Spaghetti Squash Primavera

Yields 2 servings

1 tablespoon olive oil
2 ounces white wine
1 tablespoon chopped garlic
2 tablespoons chopped shallots
8 ounces spaghetti squash
2 ounces diced carrots (blanched)
2 ounces chopped celery

2 ounces broccoli florets (roasted)
2 ounces cauliflower (roasted)
trio of baby bell peppers (roasted)
1 ounce sliced red onion
3 tablespoons chopped tarragon
3 ounces 12-month manchego cheese, shredded
cherry tomatoes, halved

Cut the squash in half, scoop out the seeds, rub olive oil over the flesh and place skin side down on baking pan. Roast in a 375 degree oven for 30–45 minutes until tender. Remove from oven and let cool, when cooled scrape out the flesh using a fork. Blanch the carrots, set aside. Roast the broccoli, cauliflower and peppers, set aside. Heat the oil in a sauté pan, add the garlic, shallots, celery and onion sauté until tender, add the carrots, broccoli, cauliflower, peppers and squash, add the wine and heat through. Divide between 2 plates. Garnish with cherry tomatoes, tarragon and cheese.

Tournedos Au Poivre

Yields 2 servings

2 tablespoons olive oil
4 3–4 ounce tournedos
2 tablespoons cracked black pepper
1 teaspoon garlic
1 tablespoon shallots
1 tablespoon Dijon mustard
2 ounces cognac
3 ounces demi-glace
2 tablespoons whole butter

Heat the oil in a medium size sauté pan. Coat the tournedos with the cracked pepper. Add to the pan cook for 3–4 minutes over medium heat. Turn steaks. Add garlic and shallots. Cook for 2 minutes or until desired doneness. Add the mustard and deglaze the pan with the cognac (when you do this there will be a flame so remove the pan from the heat add the cognac and return to the heat being very careful because it will flame up). When cognac has reduced remove steaks and keep warm. Add the demi-glace and reduce by ½. Turn off the heat and whisk in the butter. Divide the steaks between 2 plates pour the sauce over the steaks.

Desserts

Carrot Cake with Cream Cheese Frosting

Flourless Chocolate Torte

Goat Cheesecake with Lime Cream and Tropical Fruit Salsa

Chocolate Bourbon Pecan Pie

Apple Brown Betty

Chocolate Mousse

Triple Chocolate Mousse Terrine

Chocolate Pots de Creme

Crème Carmel

Vanilla Bean Crème Brûlée

Profiteroles

Lemon Berry Mille-Feuille

Lemon Panna Cotta with Blueberry Sauce

Carrot Soufflé with Cream Cheese Sauce

Oven Roasted Peaches with Honeyed Ricotta Cheese

Banana Soufflé

Chocolate Grand Marnier Soufflé

Crepes Suzette

Bananas Foster

Cherries Jubilee

Chocolate Cake with Chocolate Mousse Filling and Cream Cheese Frosting

Carrot Cake with Cream Cheese Frosting

Yields 1 9-inch cake

2 cups granulated sugar
2 cups all purpose flour
1 ¼ cups peanut oil
2 teaspoons baking powder
1 teaspoon baking soda
½ teaspoon salt
2 teaspoons cinnamon
1 teaspoon nutmeg
4 whole eggs
⅛ cup orange juice
3 cups (1 ¼ pounds) peeled grated carrots
1 cup chopped walnuts + 1 cup
1 cup raisins

Preheat oven to 375 degrees. Measure all the dry ingredients (except for second measure of walnuts) in the bowl of a kitchen aid. Measure the wet ingredients in a separate bowl. Begin mixing the dry ingredients while slowly adding the wet ingredients and mix well. Cut out 3 circles of parchment large enough to fit in the bottom of the cake pan. Place one piece of parchment in the bottom of each cake pan, and spray the sides with vegetable spray. Divide the batter evenly between the 3 pans. Place the pans in the oven and bake for 30 minutes or until a toothpick inserted in the center of the cake comes out clean. Remove from the oven and let cool. When cool remove the cake from the pan and frost. Using your hands carefully take the remaining walnuts and press them into the side of the cake. Mix orange food coloring with the remaining frosting and using a pastry bag decorate the top of the cake.

Cream Cheese Frosting
½ pound cream cheese
½ cup unsalted butter
½ teaspoon vanilla
1 pound confectionery sugar (sifted)
milk (as required)

Bring cream cheese and butter to room temperature. In the bowl of and electric mixer or kitchen aide place the cheese and butter whip on medium speed until creamy. Add the vanilla and sugar. Whip until light and fluffy, adding milk if necessary to achieve desired consistency.

Flourless Chocolate Torte

Yields 1 10-inch torte

1 pound (2 ⅓ cups) semi-sweet chocolate
1 pound unsalted butter
1 pound granulated sugar
12 whole eggs
ganache*

Preheat oven to 325 degrees. On top of a double boiler melt the chocolate, butter and sugar together. With an electric mixer or kitchen aid whip eggs for 2 ½ minutes until fluffy. Fold eggs into chocolate. Cut out a 10 inch circle of parchment paper and line the bottom of a 10 inch spring form cake pan. Wrap the outside of the pan with aluminum foil. Pour chocolate mixture into pan and place cake in a roasting pan. Fill halfway up with water, place in oven and bake for 45 minutes, rotate and continue baking for another 45 minutes. When the cake is done it should wiggle a little in the middle. Turn of the heat and keep in the oven for 1 hour. Remove from the oven and let cool at room temperature. Spread the ganache over the top and sides of the cake.

Ganache
12 ounces 54% chocolate
¾ cup heavy cream

Add chocolate and cream to a mixing bowl. Place over double boiler until chocolate has melted remove from heat and stir until chocolate and cream are combined.

Goat Cheesecake with Lime Cream and Tropical Fruit Salsa

Yields 1 9-inch cake

1 cup vanilla wafers (crushed)
¼ cup melted butter
1 pound cream cheese (room temperature)
½ cup sour cream (room temperature)
5 ounces goat cheese (room temperature)
2 egg yolks + 1 whole egg
¾ cup sugar
½ teaspoon vanilla extract
1 tablespoon lime juice

Preheat oven to 300 degrees. Add vanilla wafers to the bowl of the food processor, begin processing while adding the melted butter. Transfer cookie mixture to a greased 9-inch cake pan, compact mixture in cake pan using a flat bottomed glass. Place pan in oven for 10 minutes.

Remove and let cool. Add cream cheese to bowl of kitchen aid and begin mixing. Add the sour cream and goat cheese continue mixing until light and fluffy, scraping the side often. Add the sugar, vanilla and lime juice mix until well blended. Slowly add the eggs one at a time. Pour mixture into prepared pan. Place pan inside a larger pan and fill halfway up with water. Place cake in the oven and bake for 30 minutes turn cake around and bake for another 30 minutes until done. Turn off oven and let cheesecake sit in the oven for 1 hour. Remove from oven. Let cool. Refrigerate.

Lime Cream
2 cups heavy cream
4 tablespoons sugar
5 tablespoons lime juice

Add the cream to the bowl of a mixer, begin mixing at medium speed until peaks begin to form. Add the sugar and lime juice and continue mixing at high speed until stiff peaks form.

Tropical Fruit Salsa
Diced strawberries, pineapple and papaya tossed together.

To serve remove cake from pan and slice. Place on plate. Spoon lime cream over top and sprinkle with fruit.

Chocolate Bourbon Pecan Pie

Yields 1 9-inch pie

¾ cup semi-sweet chocolate
1 cup pecan halves
½ cup corn syrup
½ cup brown sugar
2 whole eggs
dash vanilla extract
pinch salt
1 tablespoon bourbon
¼ cup melted butter

Preheat oven to 275 degrees. Spread chocolate out evenly in unbaked pie shell. Layer pecans over chocolate and set aside. In the bowl of an electric mixer or kitchen aide, whip together the corn syrup and brown sugar on low speed. Whip together eggs, vanilla, salt and bourbon together in a small mixing bowl. Add to the syrup sugar mixture along with the melted butter. Mix until thoroughly combined. Strain mixture over chocolate and pecans in pie shell. Bake for 1 hour rotating once halfway through baking. Remove from oven and let cool to room temperature.

Apple Brown Betty

Yields 12 servings

12 apples (peeled, cored and sliced)
1 pound brown sugar
1 tablespoon cinnamon
1 teaspoon nutmeg
¼ teaspoon cloves
2 cups bread crumbs
3 cups water
juice of 2 limes
2 ounces melted butter

In a mixing bowl, mix together the sugar, cinnamon, nutmeg and cloves. Add the apples and mix well. Pour the apples into a 9"X12" casserole dish and spread the bread crumbs over the top. Add the lime juice to the water and sprinkle over the top of the bread crumbs. Cover with aluminum foil and bake for 45 minutes at 375 degrees. Remove the foil and sprinkle with the melted butter and return to the oven for 15 minutes until browned. Spoon into bowls while hot and top with vanilla bean ice cream.

Chocolate Mousse

10 ½ ounces semi-sweet chocolate
2 egg yolks
2 tablespoons brandy
2 tablespoons melted butter
4 egg whites
2 tablespoons sugar
1 cup heavy cream

Melt the chocolate in a double boiler. In a large mixing bowl whip the egg yolks, brandy and butter together. Add the chocolate and mix until thoroughly incorporated. Begin to whip egg whites in a mixer when soft peaks begin to form add the sugar and continue whipping until stiff peaks form. Fold the whites into the chocolate. Whip the heavy cream until stiff and fold into the chocolate. Place covered in the refrigerator for at least four hours to allow it to set up. Spoon or pipe into wine glasses, top with whipped cream and garnish with fresh mint.

Triple Chocolate Mousse Terrine

Yields 12 4-ounce timbale molds

White Chocolate
1 ½ cups white chocolate
6 tablespoons unsalted butter
2 tablespoons heavy cream
1 tablespoon brandy
1 egg separated

Milk Chocolate
1 cup milk chocolate
4 tablespoons unsalted butter
2 tablespoons heavy cream
1 tablespoon brandy
1 egg separated

Semi-Sweet Chocolate
1 cup semi-sweet chocolate
2 tablespoons unsalted butter
4 tablespoons heavy cream
1 tablespoon brandy
1 egg separated

Place the white chocolate, butter, cream and brandy in a stainless steel mixing bowl and melt over a double boiler. When melted stir well to combine all the ingredients remove from heat and cool slightly. Beat the yolks into the chocolate. In the bowl of a kitchen aide or electric mixer whip egg whites until stiff. Gently fold the whites into the chocolate mixture. Pour into a 4 ½ inch x 8 ½ inch loaf pan and freeze. Repeat for the milk chocolate and semi-sweet chocolate, in that order.

Chocolate Pots de Creme

Yields 6–8 servings

9 ounces chocolate chips
1 ½ cups milk
1 cup heavy cream
6 egg yolks
5 tablespoons sugar
¼ teaspoon salt

Place the chocolate in the bowl of a food processor and chop. In a saucepan whisk together the milk, cream, egg yolks, sugar and salt. Place over medium heat and cook stirring constantly with a rubber spatula until the mixture is thick enough (but not boiling) to coat the spatula (5–6 minutes). Pour the hot milk mixture over the chocolate and process until chocolate is melted and well combined and smooth. Divide the mixture between ramekins and refrigerate until set.

Crème Carmel

Yields 12 servings

caramelized sugar*
1 quart milk
8 ounces sugar
8 whole eggs
¼ teaspoon pure vanilla extract

Preheat oven to 275 degrees. Divide the caramelized sugar between 12 oven-proof ramekins. Place ramekins in a roasting pan and set aside. Place milk in saucepan and scald. In a mixing bowl mix eggs, sugar, and vanilla together. Temper the eggs with milk (pour ⅓ milk into eggs mix well and add this back to the milk) mix well. Strain through a fine mesh strainer, skim scum and froth off the top. Divide into the ramekins. Fill the pan ¾ full with hot water. Cover with foil shiny side down and cook for 1 hour and 15 minutes rotating every 15 minutes, checking to make sure the custard has set. Remove from pan and place on a sheet pan and refrigerate overnight. To serve run a knife around the edge of ramekin and invert onto serving plate, it may need a little jerk to loosen custard. Garnish with strawberries.

Caramelized Sugar
8 ounces sugar
¾ cups water

Cook the sugar in a sauté pan until completely melted and brown. Add water, stirring until mixture is completely smooth and free of lumps.

Vanilla Bean Crème Brûlée

Yields 6 servings

2 cups whole milk
2 cups heavy whipping cream
12 egg yolks

1 cup sugar plus sugar for caramelizing
½ vanilla bean

Preheat oven to 375 degrees. In a saucepot combine milk and cream, scrape vanilla bean into cream mixture, heat to a scald approximately 120 degrees. Mix sugar and eggs together. Add about 1 cup cream mixture to the eggs and whip, add this mix back to cream and mix well. Strain the mixture and skim off any foam or skin that will form. Divide between 6 brulee cups. Place cups on a sheet pan, place pan in oven, fill pan with hot water until the water is half way up the side of the cup. Cook for 30 minutes rotate and continue cooking for an additional 30 minutes. When done the custard should be some what firm, they will firm up more after they are cool, refrigerate for 2–3 hours. When ready for service, using a fine mesh strainer sprinkle sugar evenly over the top. Either place them under a broiler until the sugar is caramelized and is a golden color or use a torch and caramelize with a sweeping back and forth motion.

Profiteroles

Yields 18

1 cup of milk
4 ounces of butter
6 ounces of flour
1 cup of eggs (beaten)

Place the milk and butter into a sauce pot and bring to a boil. Add the flour and stir with a wooden spoon while continuing to cook. Keep stirring until the mix pulls away from the sides of the pot and forms a big ball. Transfer the mix to the bowl of a Kitchen-Aid. Begin mixing (with the whip attachment) on low speed until the mix has cooled, turn to medium speed while slowly adding the eggs (at one point it will look broken) continue mixing until all the eggs have been added and the mixture is a shiny medium thick paste. Place the mixture in a pastry bag with out a tip and pipe out onto parchment-lined sheet pans. They should be about the size of golf balls. Cook at 400 degrees until puffed and golden brown 10–15 minutes. Let cool. When cool slice in half and place a small scoop of gelato of choice in each profiterole and replace the top. Serve three to an order. Drizzle chocolate sauce over the top and dust with powdered sugar.

Lemon Berry Mille-Feuille

Yields 12

1 sheet puff pastry
chantilly cream
lemon sauce*
assorted berries

Preheat the oven to 400 degrees. Cut the puff pastry into equal size rectangles. Place the pastry pieces onto a parchment lined sheet pan, place metal ramekins on each corner of the pan and place another pan on top. Cook in the oven for 10–15 minutes until puffed and golden brown. Remove from the oven and let cool. When cool slice in half horizontally. Fill the bottom half with chantilly cream replace the top half and spoon lemon sauce over the top. Garnish with your choice of berries.

*Lemon Sauce
zest from 4 lemons
2 ounces of butter
1 cup lemon juice
1 cup of sugar
4 eggs

Soak the zest in the juice. Heat the sugar with the butter while stirring until the butter is fully incorporated into the sugar and the mixture will pull away from the sides of the pan and form a smooth ball. While still on the heat add the eggs one at a time, whipping rapidly until thoroughly incorporated. Add the lemon juice with the zest whipping constantly until sauce comes to a boil. The sauce should be the consistency of thin pudding. Remove from the heat and cool.

Lemon Panna Cotta with Blueberry Sauce

Yields 6 servings

2 ½ cups heavy cream
¾ cup milk
1 cup sugar

2 ½ teaspoons unflavored gelatin
½ cup lemon juice

Combine milk, cream, sugar, and gelatin in a 1 ½ quart saucepot. Place over medium heat, stirring constantly with a wire whip, heat until mixture reads 180 degrees with an instant read thermometer. Remove from heat and stir in the juice. Pour equal amounts into 6 wine glasses and refrigerate until set, approximately four hours. When set top with 3 tablespoons blueberry sauce or whatever sauce you may prefer.

Blueberry Sauce (yields 1 ½ cups)

¼ cup sugar
¾ cup cranberry juice
1 ½ teaspoons lime juice

1 tablespoon corn starch
1 ½ teaspoons dark rum
1 ¼ cup blueberries (fresh or frozen)

In a one-quart saucepan combine the sugar, cranberry juice, lime juice, corn starch and rum. Over medium heat bring to a boil, reduce heat to a simmer and simmer for 3 minutes. Add blueberries and continue simmering for 2 more minutes. Remove from heat and let cool. When cooled spoon 3 tablespoons over the top of each panna cotta. Use any leftovers for topping vanilla ice cream.

Desserts | 95

Carrot Soufflé with Cream Cheese Sauce

Yields 2 servings

Carrot Mix
1 egg
1 tablespoon brown sugar
2 tablespoons sugar
3 tablespoons salad oil
2 tablespoons honey
⅛ teaspoon salt
¾ cup flour
½ teaspoon cinnamon
¼ teaspoon nutmeg
¼ teaspoon ground cloves
¼ teaspoon baking soda
⅛ teaspoon baking powder
⅔ cup grated carrots

Place all the ingredients in the bowl of a kitchen-aid mixer. On medium speed mix well until all the ingredients are incorporated. Set aside.

Cream Cheese Pastry Cream
1 pound cream cheese
½ cup sugar
3 egg yolks

In a saucepan heat the cream cheese and ½ the sugar over low heat, stirring until melted and smooth. Slowly whip in the egg yolks and remaining sugar into cream cheese and cook over low heat until thickened. Let cool.

Souffle Batter
1 cup pastry cream
3 egg yolks
3 egg whites
½ cup sugar

In a mixing bowl whip together pastry cream and egg yolks until smooth. Add the egg whites to kitchen-aid mixer and begin whipping add the sugar and whip on high speed until stiff peaks form. Fold the whites into the yolk mixture.

Cream Cheese Sauce
1 cup cream cheese
¾ cup sugar
1 cup orange juice

In a saucepan heat the cream cheese and sugar over low heat until melted and smooth. Add orange juice and heat while stirring until smooth. Remove from heat, strain and cool.

Assembly

Preheat oven to 400 degrees. Grease soufflé cups, add sugar swirling to coat bottom and sides. Spoon carrot mixture into cups about ¼ of the way up. Fill the rest of the cup with the batter. Place in oven for 7–10 minutes until puffed and browned. Serve immediately with cream cheese sauce.

Oven Roasted Peaches with Honeyed Ricotta Cheese

Yields 6 servings

1 cup orange juice
1 vanilla bean
2 tablespoons sugar
6 peaches
¾ cup ricotta cheese
3 tablespoons honey

Preheat the oven to 375 degrees. Cut the peaches in half and remove pit. Place the peaches cut side down on a small roasting or sheet pan. Split the vanilla bean in half and scrape the vanilla into the orange juice and pour over the peaches sprinkle the sugar over the peaches and roast in the oven for 10–12 minutes until soft but firm. Remove from the oven. Set the peaches aside and reserve the juice. In a small bowl whip the ricotta and honey together. Serve the peaches warm with the juice and ricotta.

Banana Soufflé

Yields 2 servings

3 tablespoons pastry cream*
2 ounces fresh bananas
1 egg yolk
2 tablespoons creme de banana
2 egg whites
1 tablespoon sugar + 2 tablespoons

Preheat the oven to 400 degrees. Mash the banana in a mixing bowl. Stir in the pastry cream, egg yolk, creme de banana and 1 tablespoon sugar. Place the whites and 2 tablespoons sugar in the bowl of kitchen-aid. Whip on high speed until stiff peaks form. Fold the whites into the pastry cream. Grease 2 soufflé cups and add sugar swirling to coat the bottom and sides. Spoon the mix into the cups and bake for 20 minutes. Serve immediately with chocolate sauce.

*Pastry Cream
8 ounces cream cheese
¼ cup sugar
2 egg yolks

In a saucepan heat the cream cheese and ½ of the sugar over low heat, stirring until melted and smooth. Remove from heat. Stir in the egg yolks and remaining sugar. Let cool.

Chocolate Grand Marnier Soufflé

Yields 4 servings

8 ounces chocolate 54%
4 egg whites
3 egg yolks
¼ cup of sugar + 2 tablespoons
3 tablespoons Grand Marnier

Preheat oven to 400 degrees. Melt the chocolate in a double boiler stirring occasionally. In a kitchen-aid beat the egg whites with the ¼ cup of sugar until stiff. Transfer the chocolate to a mixing bowl whip 2 tablespoons sugar and Grand Marnier into the chocolate. Ad the egg yolks one at a time whipping after each addition. Fold the egg whites into the chocolate. Grease 4 souffle cups and add sugar swirling to coat the bottom and sides. Fill with soufflé mixture and bake for 20 minutes. Sift powdered sugar over the top. Serve immediately with crème anglaise.

Crème Anglaise

2 cups half and half
½ teaspoon pure vanilla extract
6 egg yolks
⅓ cup sugar

In a medium stainless steel bowl combine egg yolks and sugar with a wire whip, whip for 2 minutes. Meanwhile in a small pot bring the half and half and vanilla to a scald over medium heat, slowly add the half and half to the egg mixture, stirring gently with a wire whip. Place the mixing bowl over a pot of simmering water, using a rubber spatula stir gently until mixture reaches 180 degrees on an instant read thermometer, making sure to be constantly scraping the sides. Remove bowl from heat and place over an ice bath and continue stirring until completely cooled. Strain.

Crepes Suzette

Yields 2 servings

⅓ cup superfine sugar
juice of ½ a lemon
juice of ½ an orange
zest of ½ an orange
1 ounce Grand Marnier
3 ounces whole butter (room temp)
6 crepes
2 large scoops vanilla ice cream

Zest the orange set aside. Heat a medium size sauté pan and add the sugar. Add the juice from both the lemon and the orange. Mix well and continue mixing until the sugar begins to caramelize. Add the zest. Remove pan from flame add the Grand Marnier. Return to flame being careful as it will flame up. Stir the mixture until everything is incorporated. Add the butter and continue stirring until sauce is smooth. Add the crepes and turn to coat both sides and fold into quarters. Serve three crepes over each scoop of ice cream along with some sauce.

Crepes (yields 12 crepes)
3 eggs
1 ¼ cups milk
2 tablespoons melted butter
¼ cups + 2 tablespoons flour
½ teaspoon salt

Place all the ingredients into a mixing bowl. Mix together with a wire whip until smooth. Let rest refrigerated for 30 minutes. Heat a crepe pan or an 8 inch nonstick Teflon coated sauté pan with a little butter. Spoon enough batter into pan to just cover the bottom and swirl pan so batter is evenly distributed. Cook over low to medium heat until bubbles appear around the edges. Flip crepe over and cook 1 ½–2 minutes on the other side. Remove from the pan and let cool at room temperature. The crepes can be used immediately or stored in the refrigerator for 4–5 days or frozen for up to a month.

Bananas Foster

Yields 2 servings

2 bananas
2 tablespoons whole butter (room temperature)
½ cup brown sugar
3 teaspoons banana liqueur
5 teaspoons Myers's rum
pinch cinnamon
2 large scoops vanilla ice cream

With the peel still on slice each banana in half then again lengthwise. Remove the peel. Set aside. Heat a medium size sauté pan and add the butter, when butter has melted stir in the sugar until thoroughly combined. Add the banana liquor and bring to a simmer. Add the bananas and slightly sauté turning once to coat. Remove pan from flame and add the Myers's rum. Return to flame being careful as it will flame up. Sprinkle cinnamon over flame. When flame subsides spoon four pieces of banana with some sauce over each scoop of ice cream.

Cherries Jubilee

Yields 2 servings

1 ½ tablespoons butter (room temperature)
¼ cup brown sugar
3 teaspoons kirschwasser
1 ¾ cup drained Bing cherries (canned works fine)
5 teaspoons brandy
2 large scoops vanilla ice cream

In a medium sauté pan heat butter until melted. Stir in the brown sugar and mix well until thoroughly combined. Add the kirschwasser and simmer for 2 minutes. Add the cherries and return to a simmer. Remove the pan from the flame and add the brandy return pan to the heat being very careful because it will flame up. When flame subsides spoon the cherries over the ice cream.

Chocolate Cake with Chocolate Mousse Filling and Cream Cheese Frosting

Yields 1 9-inch cake

2 ¾ cups cake flour
3 cups sugar
1 ¼ cups cocoa
2 ¼ teaspoons baking soda
2 ¼ teaspoons baking powder
1 ½ teaspoons salt
3 eggs
1 ½ cups milk
¾ cup salad oil
1 teaspoon vanilla extract
1 ½ cups boiling water

Preheat oven to 375 degrees. Sift together all the dry ingredients into a large mixing bowl. Add a third of the dry mix to the bowl of a kitchen-aid mixer, using the wire whip attachment, begin mixing at a low speed while slowly adding the milk, when the milk is thoroughly combined add another third of the dry mix and the oil, mix until combined. Add the last of the dry ingredients and the water when thoroughly combined add the eggs and whip until the eggs are incorporated. Divide the mixture between 3 9-inch greased cake pans. Cook for 30–45 minutes until done, when a toothpick inserted comes out clean. Remove from the oven and let cool, when cooled remove from the cake pan and frost the middle two layers with chocolate mousse and frost with the cream cheese frosting.

Chocolate Mousse
10 ½ ounces semi-sweet chocolate
2 egg yolks
2 tablespoons brandy
2 tablespoons melted butter
4 egg whites
2 tablespoons sugar
1 cup heavy cream

Melt the chocolate in a double boiler. In a large mixing bowl whip the egg yolks, brandy and butter together. Add the chocolate and mix until thoroughly incorporated. Begin to whip egg whites in a mixer when soft peaks begin to form add the sugar and continue whipping until stiff peaks form. Fold the whites into the chocolate. Whip the heavy cream until stiff and fold into the chocolate. Place covered in the refrigerator for at least four hours to allow it to set up. Spoon or pipe into wine glasses, top with whipped cream and garnish with fresh mint.

Cream Cheese Frosting
½ pound cream cheese
½ cup unsalted butter
½ teaspoon vanilla
1 pound confectionery sugar (sifted)
milk (as required)

Bring cream cheese and butter to room temperature. In the bowl of an electric mixer or kitchen aide place the cheese and butter whip on medium speed until creamy. Add the vanilla and sugar. Whip until light and fluffy, adding milk if necessary to achieve desired consistency.

Stocks, Sides, Sauces, Dressings

Demi-Glace

Chicken Stock

Au Gratin Potatoes

Dauphinoise

Duchess Potatoes

Wild Rice and Mushroom Cakes

Nut Relish

Gluten-Free Flour

Spaghetti Squash

Miso Marinade

Demi-Glace

Yields 2 quarts

5 pounds beef bones
2 cups dry red wine
1 onion peeled and chopped
1 carrot peeled and chopped
1 stalk celery chopped
¼ head garlic
4 quarts water
3 bay leaves
1 ½ teaspoon thyme
½ cup tomato paste
3 tomatoes quartered
2 teaspoons salt
2 teaspoons black peppercorns

Preheat the oven to 400 degrees. Place the bones in a roasting pan, and roast for one hour. Remove the roasting pan from the oven and place the bones in a large stock pot. Place the roasting pan on the stovetop and over high heat deglaze the pan with the red wine, scraping the bottom to loosen any particles. Add the onion, carrot, celery, mushrooms, and garlic and sweat for 5 minutes. Add the vegetables to the stock pot with the remaining ingredients except the salt and peppercorns. Bring to a boil over high heat. Reduce the heat to a simmer and simmer uncovered for 4–4 ½ hours. Occasionally skim the scum that forms on top. Fifteen minutes before the stock is done add the salt and peppercorns. With a large fine mesh strainer, strain the stock, discard the bones and vegetables. Refrigerate over night. Remove any congealed fat that has formed on the surface. Reheat in stock pot and pour into ice cube trays and freeze. The stock will keep frozen for one month or thawed 3–4 days.

Chicken Stock

Yields 2 ½ quarts

1 tablespoon olive oil
1 onion peeled and chopped
1 carrot peeled and chopped
4 sticks celery chopped
½ bulb garlic
5 pounds chicken bones
3 ½ quarts cold water
3 bay leaves
1 ½ teaspoon black pepper
2 teaspoons thyme
2 teaspoons salt
1 teaspoon tarragon
1 teaspoon oregano

Wash the bones in cold water and set aside. Heat the oil in a large stock pot over high heat. Add the onion, carrot, celery and garlic, sauté, stirring occasionally for 3–5 minutes. Add the remaining ingredients, except the salt and pepper, and bring to a boil. Reduce the heat to a simmer, skim off any scum that accumulates on the surface. Simmer uncovered for 3 ½ to 4 hours. Ten minutes before the stock is done add the salt and pepper. Strain the stock through a large fine mesh strainer. Discard the bones and the vegetables. Place in the freezer until the fat congeals. Skim off any fat that has accumulated on top. Reheat stock and pour into ice cube trays and freeze. When refrigerated the stock will last 3–4 days or frozen up to a month.

Au Gratin Potatoes

Yields 8 servings

2 ¼ pounds potatoes
1 ounce whole butter
4 ounces diced yellow onion
1 ½ tablespoons chopped garlic
1 ounce flour
1 cup heavy cream
1 teaspoon salt
½ teaspoon white pepper
4 ounces grated Gruyère

Preheat oven to 400. Peel and thinly slice the potatoes. Place the potatoes in cold water and set aside. Melt the butter in a sauté pan. Add the onions and garlic and cook until soft. Stir in the flour and cook for 1 ½ minutes, add the cream, salt and pepper. Continue cooking until mixture begins to thicken. Drain the potatoes and pat dry with paper towels. Oil a baking dish and layer the potatoes in the dish. Pour the cream mixture over the potatoes and spread the cheese over the potatoes. Cover with foil and bake for 45 minutes until the potatoes are tender. Remove foil and place under broiler to brown the cheese. Allow potatoes to rest for 10 minutes before serving. Slice the potatoes into portions.

Dauphinoise

Yields 8 servings

2 ½ pounds potatoes (peeled and thinly sliced)
1 ½ cups heavy cream
1 tablespoon chopped garlic
pinch of nutmeg
1 whole egg
¼ teaspoon salt
⅛ teaspoon white pepper
½ cup grated Gruyère

Heat the oven to 375 degrees. Combine the cream, eggs, salt, pepper and nutmeg. Heat the mixture but do not let it boil. Butter a baking dish and rub it with the garlic. Layer the potatoes in the pan. Add the cream mixture and top with the cheese. Cover with foil and bake for 45 minutes until the potatoes are tender. Uncover and place under broiler to brown the cheese lightly.

Duchess Potatoes

Yields 10 servings

3 ½ pounds potatoes peeled and quartered
6 egg yolks
4 teaspoons salt
½ teaspoon white pepper

Cook the potatoes in boiling salted water until tender (being careful not to overcook). They should be tender crisp. Drain potatoes and run through a food mill. Mix in the yolks, butter and seasonings. Spoon potatoes in a pastry bag and pipe out onto parchment paper or onto plates. Let rest and cool. When ready to serve place in a 375 degree oven for 6–10 minutes until browned.

Wild Rice and Mushroom Cakes

Yields 12 cakes

1 cup cooked wild rice mixture
1 small yellow onion, finely diced
1 tablespoon minced garlic
¼ teaspoon oregano
¼ teaspoon sage
¼ teaspoon basil
¼ teaspoon thyme
4 ounces white button mushrooms, coarsely chopped
2 ½ ounces wild mushrooms (shitake, portobello; etc.), thinly sliced
1 tablespoon olive oil
1 tablespoon butter
1 ½ tablespoons Tamari
3 eggs separated, grade AA large
¼ cup gluten free flour
1 cup shredded parmesan cheese
½ teaspoon salt
¼ teaspoon black pepper

Place measured rice in a mixing bowl and set aside. Melt the butter in a sauté pan and add the onion garlic and herbs, sauté onions over medium heat until translucent. Add the onion mixture to the rice. In the same sauté pan, heat the oil and add the mushrooms and cook until golden brown, deglaze with the Tamari and cook until all the liquid has evaporated. Add the mushrooms to the bowl with the rice and onion mixture. Separate the eggs, beat the yolk until smooth, add yolks, flour, salt, pepper, and cheese to rice mixture, mix until thoroughly incorporated. Beat the egg whites with electric mixer, or Kitchen–Aid, until they form a stiff peak, but are not dry, gently fold whites into the rice mixture. Form into cakes and sauté.

Nut Relish

Yields 1 quart

8 ounces pitted black olives, drained
2 cups walnuts
8 ounces kosher dill pickles
½ cup mayonnaise
3 tablespoons honey

Place the olives in a food processor and process until smooth. Remove from the food processor and place in a mixing bowl. Repeat the procedure for the walnuts and pickles. Add the mayonnaise and honey to the mixing bowl and mix well. Refrigerate.

Gluten-Free Flour

Yields 1 quart

1 cup white rice flour
1 cup potato starch
1 cup corn starch
½ cup corn flour
½ cup tapioca flour
4 teaspoons xanthan gum

Combine all the ingredients in a mixing bowl. Mix thoroughly until all the ingredients are combined.

Spaghetti Squash

Yields 2 servings

1 spaghetti squash
olive oil
salt and pepper

Preheat oven to 400 degrees. Slice the squash in half lengthwise remove the seeds. Rub the flesh with olive oil, sprinkle with salt and pepper, and place flesh side down on a baking sheet. Place in the oven and roast for 30–45 minutes until tender. Remove from oven and let cool. When cool enough to handle scrape out the flesh using a fork.

Miso Marinade

2 tablespoons red miso
5 tablespoons sugar
1 teaspoon grated fresh ginger
½ teaspoon garlic
2 tablespoons sesame oil
1 teaspoon soy sauce
2 tablespoons mirin

In a small mixing bowl add all the ingredients and mix well.

Seasonal Menu Suggestions

Spring

English Pea Griddle Cakes

Portobello Bisque

Arugula and Beet Salad

Cedar Plank Salmon with Roasted Red Pepper Salsa

Lemon Berry Mille Feuille

Summer

Lobster Martini

Chilled Gazpacho

Sesame Seared Scallop Salad

Rainbow Trout Almondine

Oven Roasted Peaches with Honeyed Ricotta

Fall

Domaine Cheese

Roasted Butternut Squash Soup with Fig Quenelle

Hearts of Romaine

Champagne Veal

Chocolate Bourbon Pecan Pie

Winter

Steak Tartar

French Onion Soup Gratinee

Kale and Quinoa Salad

Braised Lamb Shank

Apple Brown Betty

Index

A

Acorn Squash, 70
ahi
    Ahi Salad, 43–44
    Ahi Tartar, 2–3
almonds
    Rocky Mountain Rainbow Trout
        Almondine, 68, 118
amaretto
    Acorn Squash, 70
Anaheim chilies
    Southwestern Chicken Cordon Bleu, 58
appetizers
    Ahi Tartar, 2–3
    Beef Carpaccio, 10
    Cheese Soufflé, 13
    Domaine Cheese, 14, 118
    Dungeness Crab Cakes, 4
    English Pea Griddle Cakes, 16–17, 118
    Gruyère and Parmesan Beignets, 12
    Lobster Martini, 5, 118
    Mushrooms Neptune, 6
    Roasted Red Pepper Hummus, 18
    Sautéed Brie with Caramelized Apples,
        15
    Smoked Salmon with Boursin Cheese
        Sauce on Roesti Potatoes, 7–8
    Southwestern Crab Cakes, 9
    Steak Tartar, 11, 118
apples
    Apple Brown Betty, 87, 118
    Sautéed Brie with Caramelized Apples,
        15
arugula
    Arugula and Roasted Beet Salad,
        38–39, 118
Asian pears, 46
Au Gratin Potatoes, 110

B

bacon
    Eggs Benedict, 60–61
bananas
    Banana Soufflé, 99
    Bananas Foster, 102
basil
    Herb Pesto, 75
    Orange Basil Vinaigrette, 45
    Tomato Basil Relish, 16, 17
    Tomato Bisque, 29
    Walnut Pesto, 45
beans
    French beans, 47
Béarnaise sauce
    Chicken Crepes, 55–56
    Gruyère and Parmesan Beignets, 12
beef
    Beef Carpaccio, 10
    Demi-Glace, 108
    Fettuccine Bolognese, 53
    Sautéed Miso Marinated Beef Salad,
        48–49
    Steak Tartar, 11, 118
    Tenderloin of Beef with Whisky Juniper
        Berry Sauce, 66
    Tournedos Au Poivre, 79
beets
    Arugula and Roasted Beet Salad,
        38–39, 118
    Kale and Quinoa Salad, 40
    Orange Beet Dressing, 38
    Roasted Beet Gazpacho, 35
    roasting, 39
berries
    Blueberry Sauce, 95
    Cherries Jubilee, 103
    Crème Carmel, 91
    Fig Quenelle, 24, 118

Goat Cheesecake with Line Cream and
    Tropical Fruit Salsa, 85
Lemon Berry Mille-Feuille, 94, 118
Lemon Panna Cotta with Blueberry
    Sauce, 95
Lobster Martini, 5
Spinach and Tofu Salad, 41
Sun-Dried Cherry Sauce, 65
Whisky Juniper Berry Sauce, 66
blueberries
    Blueberry Sauce, 95
Bolognese sauce
    Fettuccine Bolognese, 53
    Portobello Bolognese, 74
Bordelaise, Vegetarian, 76–77
bourbon
    Chocolate Bourbon Pecan Pie, 86, 118
Boursin cheese
    Smoked Salmon with Boursin Cheese
        Sauce on Roesti Potatoes, 7–8
Braised Lamb Shank, 64, 118
brandy
    Cherries Jubilee, 103
    Chocolate Mousse, 88, 104
    Sweet Potato Bisque, 30
    Triple Chocolate Mousse Terrine, 89
Brie cheese
    Sautéed Brie with Caramelized Apples, 15
Brown Betty, Apple, 87, 118
butternut squash
    Roasted Butternut Squash Soup with
        Fig Quenelle, 24, 118

C

cakes
    Carrot Cake with Cream Cheese
        Frosting, 82
    Chocolate Cake with Chocolate Mousse
        Filling and Cream Cheese
        Frosting, 104–105
    Wild Rice and Mushroom Cakes, 113
Canadian bacon
    Hash Browns, 60–61
capellini pasta, 43

capers
    Chicken Piccata, 57
    Steak Tartar, 11
Caramelized Sugar, 91
carrots
    Carrot Cake with Cream Cheese
        Frosting, 82
    Carrot Soufflé with Cream Cheese
        Sauce, 96–97
    Fettuccine Bolognese, 53
    Kale and Quinoa Salad, 40
    mire poix, 64
    Portobello Bolognese, 74
    Sautéed Miso Marinated Beef Salad, 48–49
    Scallop Salad, 46
    Spaghetti Squash Primavera, 78
    Vegetarian Split Pea Soup, 25
Cedar Plank Salmon with Roasted Red
    Pepper Salsa, 67, 118
champagne
    Champagne Veal, 52, 118
Chantilly cream
    Lemon Berry Mille-Feuille, 94
cheese
    Au Gratin Potatoes, 110
    Carrot Soufflé with Cream Cheese
        Sauce, 96–97
    Cheese Soufflé, 13
    Cream Cheese Frosting, 82, 104–105
    Cream Cheese Pastry Cream, 96, 99
    Dauphinoise, 111
    Domaine Cheese, 14, 118
    English Pea Griddle Cakes, 15
    French Onion Soup Gratinee, 22, 118
    Goat Cheesecake with Lime Cream and
        Tropical Fruit Salsa, 84–85
    Gruyère and Parmesan Beignets, 12
    Hearts of Romaine Salad, 47
    Mushrooms Neptune, 6
    Oven Roasted Peaches with Honeyed
        Ricotta Cheese, 98
    Sautéed Brie with Caramelized Apples, 15

Smoked Salmon with Boursin Cheese Sauce on Roesti Potatoes, 7–8
Southwestern Chicken Cordon Bleu, 58
Walnut Pesto, 45
Wild Rice and Mushroom Cakes, 113

cheesecake
Goat Cheesecake with Lime Cream and Tropical Fruit Salsa, 84–85

cherries
Cherries Jubilee, 103
Sun-Dried Cherry Sauce, 65

chicken
Chicken Crepes, 55–56
Chicken Marsala, 59
Chicken Piccata, 57
Chicken Stock, 109
Hearts of Romaine Salad, 47
Southwestern Chicken Cordon Bleu, 58

chilies
Southwestern Chicken Cordon Bleu, 58
Southwestern Crab Cakes, 9
Sweet Corn Soup with Smoked Chili Cream, 23

Chilled Gazpacho, 34, 118
Chilled Vichyssoise, 31

chipotle
Sweet Corn Soup with Smoked Chili Cream, 9

chocolate
Chocolate Bourbon Pecan Pie, 86, 118
Chocolate Cake with Chocolate Mousse Filling and Cream Cheese Frosting, 104–105
Chocolate Grand Marnier Soufflé, 99
Chocolate Mousse, 88, 104
Chocolate Pots de Creme, 90
Flourless Chocolate Torte, 83
Ganache, 83
Profiteroles, 93
Triple Chocolate Mousse Terrine, 89

cilantro pesto
Beef Carpaccio, 10

Citrus Vinaigrette, Oriental, 43, 44

cognac
Lobster Bisque, 26–27

Tournedos Au Poivre, 79

corn
Sweet Corn Soup with Smoked Chili Cream, 23

crab cakes
Dungeness Crab Cakes, 4
Southwestern Crab Cakes, 9

cream cheese
Carrot Soufflé with Cream Cheese Sauce, 96–97
Chocolate Cake with Chocolate Mousse Filling and Cream Cheese Frosting, 104–105
Cream Cheese Frosting, 82, 105
Cream Cheese Pastry Cream, 96, 99
Domaine Cheese, 14, 118
Goat Cheesecake with Lime Cream and Tropical Fruit Salsa, 84–85
Mushrooms Neptune, 6

Creamed Pine Nuts, 65
Creamy Tomato Sauce, 72
Crème Anglaise, 100
Crème Brûlée, Vanilla Bean, 92
Crème Carmel, 91

crepes
Chicken Crepes, 55–56
Crepes Suzette, 101

D

Dauphinoise, 111
Demi-Glace, 108

desserts
Apple Brown Betty, 87, 118
Banana Soufflé, 99
Bananas Foster, 102
Carrot Cake with Cream Cheese Frosting, 82
Carrot Soufflé with Cream Cheese Sauce, 95, 96–97
Cherries Jubilee, 103
Chocolate Bourbon Pecan Pie, 86, 118
Chocolate Cake with Chocolate Mousse Filling and Cream Cheese Frosting, 104–105
Chocolate Grand Marnier Soufflé, 100

Chocolate Mousse, 88
Chocolate Pots de Creme, 90
Crème Carmel, 91
Crepes Suzette, 101
Flourless Chocolate Torte, 83
Goat Cheesecake with Line Cream and Tropical Fruit Salsa, 84–85
Lemon Berry Mille-Feuille, 94, 118
Lemon Panna Cotta with Blueberry Sauce, 95
Oven Roasted Peaches with Honeyed Ricotta Cheese, 98, 118
Profiteroles, 93
Triple Chocolate Mousse Terrine, 89
Vanilla Bean Crème Brûlée, 92
Dijon Vinaigrette, 47
Domaine Cheese, 14, 118
dressings, salad. *See* salad dressings
Duchess Potatoes, 112
Dungeness Crab Cakes, 4

E

Eggplant Parmesan, 71–72
eggs
    Egg Wash, 72, 73, 76
    Eggs Benedict, 60–61
    Eggs Florentine, 62–63
English muffins
    Eggs Benedict, 60–61
    Eggs Florentine, 62–63
English Pea Griddle Cakes, 16–17, 118
entrees
    Acorn Squash, 70
    Braised Lamb Shank, 64, 118
    Cedar Plank Salmon with Roasted Red Pepper Salsa, 67, 118
    Champagne Veal, 52, 118
    Chicken Crepes, 55–56
    Chicken Marsala, 59
    Chicken Piccata, 57
    Eggplant Parmesan, 71–72
    Eggs Benedict, 60–61
    Eggs Florentine, 62–63
    Fettuccine Bolognese, 53
    Madame Oak Creek, 54
    Portobello Bolognese, 74
    Roasted Pork Tenderloin with Sun-Dried Cherry Sauce and Creamed Pine Nuts, 65
    Rocky Mountain Rainbow Trout Almondine, 68, 118
    Sautéed Sand Dabs au Meunière, 69
    Seitan Wellington, 75–77
    Southwestern Chicken Cordon Bleu, 58
    Spaghetti Squash Primavera, 78
    Tenderloin of Beef with Whisky Juniper Berry Sauce, 66
    Tournedos Au Poivre, 79
    Wild Mushroom Strudel, 73
Espagnole Sauce, Vegetarian, 76

F

feta cheese
    Beef Carpaccio, 10
    Wild Mushroom Strudel, 73
Fettuccine Bolognese, 53
Fig Quenelle, 24, 118
fish and seafood
    Ahi Salad, 43–44
    Ahi Tartar, 2–3
    Cedar Plank Salmon with Roasted Red Pepper Salsa, 67, 118
    Dungeness Crab Cakes, 4
    Lobster Bisque, 26–27
    Lobster Martini, 5, 118
    Rocky Mountain Rainbow Trout Almondine, 68, 118
    Salmon Salad, 45
    Sautéed Sand Dabs au Meunière, 69
    Scallop Salad, 46, 118
    Smoked Salmon with Boursin Cheese Sauce on Roesti Potatoes, 7–8
    Southwestern Crab Cakes, 9
Flour, Gluten-Free, 115
French beans
    Hearts of Romaine Salad, 47
French Onion Soup Gratinee, 22, 118
frostings
    Cream Cheese Frosting, 82, 105

fruit
    Apple Brown Betty, 87, 118
    Asian pears, 46
    Banana Soufflé, 99
    Bananas Foster, 102
    Blueberry Sauce, 95
    Crème Carmel, 91
    Goat Cheesecake with Line Cream and Tropical Fruit Salsa, 85
    Lemon Sauce, 94
    Lime Cream, 85
    Orange Basil Vinaigrette, 45
    Oriental Citrus Vinaigrette, 43, 44
    Oven Roasted Peaches with Honeyed Ricotta Cheese, 98, 118
    Roasted Butternut Squash Soup with Fig Quenelle, 24
    Salmon Salad, 45
    Sautéed Brie with Caramelized Apples, 15
    Sun-Dried Cherry Sauce, 65
    Tropical Fruit Salsa, 85

G
Ganache, 83
gazpacho soups
    Chilled Gazpacho, 34, 118
    Roasted Beet Gazpacho, 35
ginger
    Ahi Salad, 43
    Ginger Mustard Vinaigrette, 48
    Miso Marinade, 117
    Scallop Salad, 46
Gluten-Free Flour, 115
goat cheese
    Goat Cheesecake with Line Cream and Tropical Fruit Salsa, 84–85
Grand Marnier
    Chocolate Grand Marnier Soufflé, 100
    Crepes Suzette, 101
grapefruit
    Lobster Martini, 5
griddle cakes
    English Pea Griddle Cakes, 16–17, 118

Gruyère cheese
    Au Gratin Potatoes, 110
    Cheese Soufflé, 13
    Dauphinoise, 111
    French Onion Soup Gratinee, 22, 118
    Gruyère and Parmesan Beignets, 12

H
ham
    Southwestern Chicken Cordon Bleu, 58
Hash Browns, 60, 62
Hazelnut Vinaigrette, 41, 42
Hearts of Romaine Salad, 47, 118
Herb Pesto, 75
Hollandaise sauce
    Chicken Crepes, 56
    Dungeness Crab Cakes, 4
    Eggs Benedict, 60–61
    Eggs Florentine, 62–63
    Gruyère and Parmesan Beignets, 12
    Southwestern Crab Cakes, 9
honey
    Oven Roasted Peaches with Honeyed Ricotta Cheese, 98
hummus
    Roasted Red Pepper Hummus, 18

I
ice cream
    Bananas Foster, 102
    Cherries Jubilee, 103

J
juniper berries
    Whisky Juniper Berry Sauce, 66

K
kale
    Kale and Quinoa Salad, 40, 118
kirschwasser
    Cherries Jubilee, 103

L
lamb
    Braised Lamb Shank, 64, 118

lemons
    Lemon Berry Mille-Feuille, 94, 118
    Lemon Panna Cotta with Blueberry Sauce, 95
    Lemon Sauce, 94
lettuce
    Hearts of Romaine Salad, 47, 118
Lime Cream, 85
lobster
    Lobster Bisque, 26–27
    Lobster Martini, 5, 118
    Mushrooms Neptune, 6

M

macadamia nuts
    Beef Carpaccio, 10
Madame Oak Creek, 54
Maggi seasonings, 54, 75
Manchego cheese
    Beef Carpaccio, 10
    Hearts of Romaine Salad, 47
    Spaghetti Squash Primavera, 78
marinades
    Miso Marinade, 48, 117
    Scallop Salad, 46
    Soy Marinade, 43, 44
Marsala sauce
    Chicken Marsala, 59
Mascarpone cheese
    English Pea Griddle Cakes, 16–17
meat dishes
    Beef Carpaccio, 10
    Braised Lamb Shank, 64
    Champagne Veal, 52, 188
    Demi-Glace, 108
    Fettuccine Bolognese, 53
    Madame Oak Creek, 54
    Roasted Pork Tenderloin with Sun-Dried Cherry Sauce and Creamed Pine Nuts, 65
    Sautéed Miso Marinated Beef Salad, 48–49
    Steak Tartar, 11, 118
    Tenderloin of Beef with Whisky Juniper Berry Sauce, 66
    Tournedos Au Poivre, 79
Mille-Feuille, Lemon Berry, 94, 118
mire poix, 64
miso
    Miso Marinade, 48, 117
    Sautéed Miso Marinated Beef Salad, 48–49
mousses
    Chocolate Cake with Chocolate Mousse Filling and Cream Cheese Frosting, 104–105
    Chocolate Mousse, 88, 104
    Triple Chocolate Mousse Terrine, 89
mushrooms
    Acorn Squash, 70
    Champagne Veal, 52
    Chicken Crepes, 55–56
    Chicken Marsala, 59
    Madam Oak Creek, 54
    Mushrooms Duxelles, 75
    Mushrooms Neptune, 6
    Portobello Bisque, 28, 118
    Portobello Bolognese, 74
    Seitan Wellington, 75
    Spinach and Wild Mushroom Salad, 42
    Wild Mushroom Strudel, 73
    Wild Rice and Mushroom Cakes, 113
mustard
    Dijon Vinaigrette, 47
    Ginger Mustard Vinaigrette, 48

N

noodles. *See* pasta and noodles
nuts
    Beef Carpaccio, 10
    Creamed Pine Nuts, 65
    Hazelnut Vinaigrette, 42
    Herb Pesto, 75
    Kale and Quinoa Salad, 40
    Nut Relish, 114
    Roasted Pork Tenderloin with Sun-Dried Cherry Sauce and Creamed Pine Nuts, 65
    Walnut Pesto, 45

O

olives
  Nut Relish, 114
onions
  French Onion Soup Gratinee, 22, 118
oranges
  Orange Basil Vinaigrette, 45
  Orange Beet Dressing, 38
  Salmon Salad, 45
  Spinach and Tofu Salad, 41
Oriental Citrus Vinaigrette, 43, 44
Oven Roasted Peaches with Honeyed Ricotta Cheese, 98, 118

P

panna cotta
  Lemon Panna Cotta with Blueberry Sauce, 95
papaya
  Goat Cheesecake with Line Cream and Tropical Fruit Salsa, 85
Parmesan cheese
  Cheese Soufflé, 13
  Eggplant Parmesan, 71–72
  French Onion Soup Gratinee, 22, 118
  Gruyère and Parmesan Beignets, 12
  Walnut Pesto, 45
  Wild Rice and Mushroom Cakes, 113
pasta and noodles
  Ahi Salad, 43
  Fettuccine Bolognese, 53
  Madame Oak Creek, 54
  Portobello Bolognese, 74
pastry cream
  Cream Cheese Pastry Cream, 96, 99
peaches
  Oven Roasted Peaches with Honeyed Ricotta Cheese, 98, 118
pears
  Scallop Salad, 46
peas
  English Pea Griddle Cakes, 16–17
pecans
  Chocolate Bourbon Pecan Pie, 86, 188
  Spiced Pecans, 33
  Sweet Potato Vichyssoise, 32–33
peppers. *See also* chilies
  Acorn Squash, 70
  Chilled Gazpacho, 34, 118
  Dungeness Crab Cakes, 4
  Roasted Beet Gazpacho, 35
  Roasted Red Pepper Cream, 58
  Roasted Red Pepper Hummus, 18
  Roasted Red Pepper Salsa, 67
  Southwestern Crab Cakes, 9
  Spaghetti Squash Primavera, 78
pesto
  Beef Carpaccio, 10
  Herb Pesto, 75
  Walnut Pesto, 45
pickles
  Nut Relish, 114
pies
  Chocolate Bourbon Pecan Pie, 86, 118
pine nuts
  Creamed Pine Nuts, 65
  Herb Pesto, 75
  Kale and Quinoa Salad, 40
pineapple
  Goat Cheesecake with Line Cream and Tropical Fruit Salsa, 85
piñon nuts. *See* pine nuts
poblano chilies
  Southwestern Crab Cakes, 9
ponzu
  Ahi Tartar, 2, 3
pork
  Roasted Pork Tenderloin with Sun-Dried Cherry Sauce and Creamed Pine Nuts, 65
portobello mushrooms
  Portobello Bisque, 28, 118
  Portobello Bolognese, 74
potatoes
  Au Gratin Potatoes, 110
  Chilled Vichyssoise, 31
  Dauphinoise, 111
  Duchess Potatoes, 112
  Hash Browns, 60, 62

Smoked Salmon with Boursin Cheese Sauce on Roesti Potatoes, 7–8
poultry. *See* chicken
Profiteroles, 93
Provolone cheese
    French Onion Soup Gratinee, 22, 118
    Wild Mushroom Strudel, 73

Q
quinoa
    Kale and Quinoa Salad, 40, 118

R
rainbow trout
    Rocky Mountain Rainbow Trout Almondine, 68, 118
relishes
    Nut Relish, 114
    Tomato Basil Relish, 16, 17
ricotta cheese
    Oven Roasted Peaches with Honeyed Ricotta Cheese, 98, 118
Roasted Beet Gazpacho, 35
Roasted Butternut Squash Soup with Fig Quenelle, 24, 118
Roasted Pork Tenderloin with Sun-Dried Cherry Sauce and Creamed Pine Nuts, 65
Roasted Red Pepper Cream, 58
Roasted Red Pepper Hummus, 18
Roasted Red Pepper Salsa, 67
Rocky Mountain Rainbow Trout Almondine, 68, 118
Roesti potatoes
    Smoked Salmon with Boursin Cheese Sauce on Roesti Potatoes, 7–8
romaine lettuce
    Hearts of Romaine Salad, 47, 118
Roquefort cheese
    Domaine Cheese, 14, 118
Roux, 27, 55
rum
    Bananas Foster, 102
    Blueberry Sauce, 95

Roasted Butternut Squash Soup with Fig Quenelle, 24

S
salad dressings
    Dijon Vinaigrette, 47
    Ginger Mustard Vinaigrette, 48
    Hazelnut Vinaigrette, 41, 42
    Orange Basil Vinaigrette, 45
    Orange Beet Dressing, 38
    Oriental Citrus Vinaigrette, 43, 44
    Sesame Vinaigrette, 46
salads
    Ahi Salad, 43–44
    Arugula and Roasted Beet Salad, 38–39, 118
    Hearts of Romaine, 47, 118
    Kale and Quinoa Salad, 40, 118
    Salmon Salad, 45
    Sautéed Miso Marinated Beef Salad, 48–49
    Scallop Salad, 46, 118
    Spinach and Tofu Salad, 41
    Spinach and Wild Mushroom Salad, 42
salmon
    Cedar Plank Salmon with Roasted Red Pepper Salsa, 67, 118
    Salmon Salad, 45
    Smoked Salmon with Boursin Cheese Sauce on Roesti Potatoes, 7–8
salsas
    Lobster Martini, 5
    Roasted Red Pepper Salsa, 67
    Tropical Fruit Salsa, 85
sand dabs
    Sautéed Sand Dabs au Meunière, 69
sauces
    Béarnaise Sauce, 12, 56
    Blueberry Sauce, 95
    Bolognese Sauce, 53, 74
    Boursin Cheese Sauce, 7–8
    Chicken Marsala, 59
    Cream Cheese Sauce, 96–97
    Creamy Tomato Sauce, 72
    Hollandaise Sauce, 4, 9, 56, 61, 62–63

Lemon Sauce, 94
Madam Oak Creek Sauce, 54
Piccata Sauce, 57
Roasted Red Pepper Cream, 58
Sun-Dried Cherry Sauce, 65
tartar dressing, 2, 3
Vegetarian Bordelaise, 76–77
Vegetarian Espagnole Sauce, 76
Whisky Juniper Berry Sauce, 66

sausage
    Fettuccine Bolognese, 53

Sautéed Brie with Caramelized Apples, 15
Sautéed Miso Marinated Beef Salad, 48–49
Sautéed Sand Dabs au Meunière, 69
Scallop Salad, 46, 118

scallopini
    Madame Oak Creek, 54

seafood. *See* fish and seafood
Seitan Wellington, 75–77

sesame seed tuiles
    Ahi Tartar, 2, 3
    Sautéed Miso Marinated Beef Salad, 48–49

Sesame Vinaigrette, 46
Smoked Chili Cream, 23
Smoked Salmon with Boursin Cheese Sauce on Roesti Potatoes, 7–8

soufflés
    Banana Soufflé, 99
    Carrot Soufflé with Cream Cheese Sauce, 96–97
    Cheese Soufflé, 13
    Chocolate Grand Marnier Soufflé, 100

soups
    Chilled Gazpacho, 34, 118
    Chilled Vichyssoise, 31
    French Onion Soup Gratinee, 22, 118
    Lobster Bisque, 26–27
    Portobello Bisque, 28, 118
    Roasted Beet Gazpacho, 35
    Roasted Butternut Squash Soup with Fig Quenelle, 24, 118
    Sweet Corn Soup with Smoked Chili Cream, 23
    Sweet Potato Bisque, 30
    Sweet Potato Vichyssoise, 32–33
    Tomato Bisque, 29
    Vegetarian Split Pea Soup, 25

Southwestern Crab Cakes, 9
Soy Marinade, 43, 44

spaghetti squash
    Spaghetti Squash, 116
    Spaghetti Squash Primavera, 78

Spiced Pecans, 33

spinach
    Eggs Florentine, 62–63
    Spinach and Tofu Salad, 41
    Spinach and Wild Mushroom Salad, 42

Split Pea Soup, Vegetarian, 25

squash
    Acorn Squash, 70
    Roasted Butternut Squash Soup with Fig Quenelle, 24, 118
    Spaghetti Squash, 116
    Spaghetti Squash Primavera, 78

Steak Tartar, 11, 118

stocks
    Chicken Stock, 109
    Demi-Glace, 108

strawberries
    Crème Carmel, 91
    Goat Cheesecake with Line Cream and Tropical Fruit Salsa, 85
    Spinach and Tofu Salad, 41

strudel
    Wild Mushroom Strudel, 73

sugar, caramelized, 91
Sun-Dried Cherry Sauce, 65
Sweet Corn Soup with Smoked Chili Cream, 23

sweet potatoes
    Sweet Potato Bisque, 30
    Sweet Potato Vichyssoise, 32–33

Swiss cheese
    French Onion Soup Gratinee, 22, 118

T

tarragon reduction
    Chicken Crepes, 56
    Gruyère and Parmesan Beignets, 12

tartar dressing
    Ahi Tartar, 2, 3
Tenderloin of Beef with Whisky Juniper
    Berry Sauce, 66
toast points
    Beef Carpaccio, 10
tofu
    Seitan Wellington, 75–77
    Spinach and Tofu Salad, 41
    Vegetarian Bordelaise Sauce, 76–77
tomatoes
    Chilled Gazpacho, 34
    Creamy Tomato Sauce, 72
    peeling, 29
    Roasted Beet Gazpacho, 35
    Tomato Basil Relish, 16, 17
    Tomato Bisque, 29
    Tomato Petals, 47
tortes
    Flourless Chocolate Torte, 83
Tournedos Au Poivre, 79
Triple Chocolate Mousse Terrine, 89
Tropical Fruit Salsa, 85
trout
    Rocky Mountain Rainbow Trout
        Almondine, 68, 118
tuiles
    Ahi Tartar, 2, 3
    Sautéed Miso Marinated Beef Salad,
        48–49
tuna
    Ahi Salad, 43–44
    Ahi Tartar, 2–3

V

Vanilla Bean Crème Brûlée, 92
veal
    Champagne Veal, 52, 118
    Fettuccine Bolognese, 53
    Madame Oak Creek, 54
vegetarian dishes
    Acorn Squash, 70
    Apple Brown Betty, 87, 118
    Arugula and Roasted Beet Salad,
        38–39, 118

Au Gratin Potatoes, 110
Banana Soufflé, 99
Bananas Foster, 102
Carrot Cake with Cream Cheese
    Frosting, 82
Carrot Soufflé with Cream Cheese
    Sauce, 96–97
Cheese Soufflé, 13
Cherries Jubilee, 103
Chilled Gazpacho, 34, 118
Chocolate Bourbon Pecan Pie, 86, 118
Chocolate Cake with Chocolate Mousse
    Filling and Cream Cheese
    Frosting, 104–105
Chocolate Grand Marnier Soufflé, 100
Chocolate Mousse, 88
Chocolate Pots de Creme, 90
Crème Carmel, 91
Crepes Suzette, 101
Dauphinoise, 111
Domaine Cheese, 14, 118
Duchess Potatoes, 112
Eggplant Parmesan, 71–72
Eggs Benedict, 60–61
Eggs Florentine, 62–63
English Pea Griddle Cakes, 16–17, 118
Flourless Chocolate Torte, 83
Gluten-Free Flour, 115
Goat Cheesecake with Lime Cream and
    Tropical Fruit Salsa, 84–85
Gruyère and Parmesan Beignets, 12
Hearts of Romaine, 47, 118
Kale and Quinoa Salad, 40, 118
Lemon Berry Mille-Feuille, 94, 118
Lemon Panna Cotta with Blueberry
    Sauce, 95
Miso Marinade, 117
Nut Relish, 114
Oven Roasted Peaches with Honeyed
    Ricotta Cheese, 98, 118
Portobello Bisque, 28, 118
Portobello Bolognese, 74
Profiteroles, 93
Roasted Beet Gazpacho, 35

Roasted Butternut Squash Soup with Fig Quenelle, 24, 118
Roasted Red Pepper Hummus, 18
Sautéed Brie with Caramelized Apples, 15
Seitan Wellington, 75–77
Spaghetti Squash, 116
Spaghetti Squash Primavera, 78
Spinach and Tofu Salad, 41
Spinach and Wild Mushroom Salad, 42
Sweet Corn Soup with Smoked Chili Cream, 23
Sweet Potato Bisque, 30
Sweet Potato Vichyssoise, 32–33
Tomato Bisque, 29
Triple Chocolate Mouse Terrine, 89
Vanilla Bean Crème Brûlée, 92
Vegetarian Bordelaise Sauce, 76–77
Vegetarian Espagnole Sauce, 76
Vegetarian Split Pea Soup, 25
Wild Mushroom Strudel, 73
Wild Rice and Mushroom Cakes, 113

vichyssoise
    Chilled Vichyssoise, 31
    Sweet Potato Vichyssoise, 32–33

W

walnuts
    Nut Relish, 114
    Walnut Pesto, 45

whisky
    Whisky Juniper Berry Sauce, 66

wild mushrooms
    Chicken Marsala, 59
    Spinach and Wild Mushroom Salad, 42
    Wild Mushroom Strudel, 73
    Wild Rice and Mushroom Cakes, 113

Wild Rice and Mushroom Cakes, 113

Y

yams
    Sweet Potato Bisque, 30
    Sweet Potato Vichyssoise, 32–33

Made in the USA
Columbia, SC
07 February 2019